The
GUEST
from
HELL

The
GUEST
from
HELL

Alistair Sampson

Illustrated by
Annie Tempest

ORION

Text © Alistair Sampson 2000
Illustrations © Annie Tempest 2000
All rights reserved

The right of Alistair Sampson and Annie Tempest to be identified
as the author and illustrator of this work
has been asserted by them in accordance with
the Copyright, Designs and Patents Act 1988.

First published in Great Britain in 2000 by
Orion Media
An imprint of Orion Books Ltd
Orion House, 5 Upper St Martin's Lane, London WC2H 9EA

A CIP catalogue record for this book is available
from the British Library

ISBN 0 75284 106 8

Typeset by Selwood Systems, Midsomer Norton
Printed in Great Britain by
Butler & Tanner Ltd, Frome and London

To Jo, a gal – one of the Wandsworth Ballingals – who, not content with presiding over my antique emporium*, has also found time in between lunches, hair appointments, visits to the dressmaker in Cheam, private telephone calls, long weekends, waiting for the plumber – I could go on – to type every word of this mish-mash of pretentious twaddle[†] single-handed (I have offered to pay for lessons). As we went along she shared with me her views on the quality of the material. Despite all, I never lost heart.

    * Alistair Sampson Antiques
      120 Mount Street
      London
      W1K 3NN
      Telephone: 020 7409 1799
      Fax: 020 7409 7717
      Website: www.alistairsampson.com
      Email: info@alistairsampson.com

      Firm's motto: 'God loves a cheerful spender'

   [†] Critics please note, you read it here first.

The Guest in Hell

Foreword by Alan Coren

Oh God, a snowdrop has appeared outside my window. Well, probably a snowdrop, could be an anaemic crocus, I am not a man to run to with floral queries, but whatever it is, it is a harbinger, that much I do know. It has shoved itself through the lawn with an announcement. The heart plummets. Any morning now, I shall begin receiving letters with rural postmarks, the general thrust of which will be to invite me to rise up and come away, for, lo, the winter is past, the rain is over and gone, the flowers appear on the earth, the time of the singing of the birds is come, and the voice of the turtle is heard in the land.

The turtle will want me and my wife to join it for a weekend in the country. The turtle either lives in the country or owns a weekend bolt-hole there, as the result of either of which it has to have company or it will go barmy. That is not to say it isn't a worthy turtle, generous, convivial, hospitable to a fault; many turtles, indeed, buy places in the country primarily because they wish not merely to entertain more chums than can be accommodated in titchy town-houses, but also to entertain them more liberally. For you cannot chuck another log into the inglenook of a smokeless Belgravia mews, nor dance the Gay Gordons the length and breadth of a Hampstead flat, nor take your horse for a brisk canter over Notting Hill and return to suck up Bollinger with three hundred neighbours on a Kensington balcony, while the ox turns, crisping, in the microwave.

The fact that, at the thought of country weekends, my heart aches and a drowsy numbness pains my sense thus has nothing whatever to do with the turtles, who are heavenly hosts. It has everything to do with me, who is a hellish guest. You will, however, not find me in the rich pages that follow, either in Alistair Sampson's shimmering prose or in Annie Tempest's delightful drawings, because I am not – at least I try not to be – a guest from hell. I am a guest *in* hell.

I travel well, but unless I am able to command the environment to which I have travelled, I transplant badly. Dispatched to a painstakingly selected hotel, knowing what I have planned for the weekend and with whom and in what clothes, and that there are fawning staff at my every beck to satisfy my every whim in return for my every penny, and, come Friday evening, I shall let Cricklewood dwindle in my wing-mirror with an optimistic heart. I shall know where I stand, and, more important, where I shall be standing later.

I know I shall not be standing in a corridor at 3am between my room and the bathroom it turns out not to have ensuite, inadequately clad in my wife's peignoir because I did not bring my dressing gown, and (a) not knowing which of these doors has a bathroom behind it, (b) whether my host's Alsatian, which has just materialised at the far end of the corridor, had a good enough sniff of me when I arrived to distinguish me from a prowling transvestite wondering which door conceals the family silver, or (c) if not, whether it would be better to stand stock still or run like hell.

Even at 6am the scenario would be little better. I have woken with a sandpaper throat, thanks both to being forced to shout off-key round a piano for some hours and to drinking in a corner for some more hours to eradicate my previous embarrassment, and what I am now desperate for is a cuppa, but where do they keep the tea, where do they keep the sugar, the milk must be in the fridge, yes it is, no it's not, it's on the floor now, and, oh look, the Al has heard the crash, a prowling transvestite is stealing the family food . . .

Turtles don't invariably keep an Alsatian, mind. They do not need one if they have a burglar alarm, wired to alert not only the sleeping household to the fact that a drunken cross-dresser has just walked through an infra-red beam, but also the local constabulary, who, with any luck, will arrive any minute now with their own Alsatian.

Not that a hellish guest requires such disasters in order to have a hellish time. He may have woken at 6am and done nothing more than stare out of a window for three hours, wondering what time the family has breakfast, finally creeping downstairs to discover it has it at 7.30 and that Mrs Daily, who does for the turtles, has just finished shaking the tablecloth out. True, there is a stiff rasher of cold bacon left in a frying-pan, but there is also an Alsatian looking at it. Upon returning to his room to tell his wife she was absolutely right, countryfolk do indeed breakfast early, sorry, he sees (a) that she is not there, and (b) that, from the window, the turtles and all their guests are yomping across a paddock towards a distant wood. Knowing that a good guest would be of their number, the hellish guest hurtles off in apologetic pursuit.

The paddock, up close, proves to have the consistency of the Somme salient, but it is now too late to go back and ask Mrs Daily if the turtles keep wellies for guests who forgot to pack them, for he is in mud stepp'd in so far that, should he wade no more, returning were as tedious as go o'er. He eventually squelches up to the party at the exact moment they are entering the wood and thus poised to begin excitedly identifying things. "Good God, isn't that *Argybargy condominium* over there, how incredible, oh look, what a splendid example of Old Man's Bum, down there near the clump of *Copious mucus*, I've never seen such a ..." Others, meanwhile, prefer to search the skies: "It can't be, where are my field glasses, yes, by heaven, it is, it's a Snotty Falcon, there must be a colony of bandy voles round here, they're the only prey a Snotty ..."

The hellish guest can contribute nothing whatever to this. Raised in an environment where anything trying to grow through a crack in the patio fell to the blowlamp before it could burgeon into identifiability, and unable to distinguish between a sparrow and a starling unless they happen to be lying dead together so that one can be seen to be larger than the other, he can do nothing but pray some litter-lout has ambled this way and given him the opportunity to cry: "I say, isn't that a Snickers wrapper?" before anyone else spots it.

Everyone now yomps home for lunch, duly banging on about country air and appetites, none of them more ravenous than the breakfastless guest. And lunch is rather special. You can tell this right away from all the nudging and winking by the turtles: for lunch is one of Mrs Daily's famous game pies, and Mr Daily is, well, no names, no pack drill, a bit of a poacher, ha-ha, don't ask what's in it, just tuck in. The pie is the size of a suitcase. Beneath his triangular slab, the hellish guest can see strange rhomboid chunks, arcane organs, little limbs. Is this Mrs Daily's famous gull-and-weasel, perhaps, her famous toe-and-bladder, her ...

After lunch, while his wife helps with the washing-up by putting everything away in cupboards from which they have sub-sequently to be removed by people who know where they go, the guest can think of no other way of doing his bit than by asking whether anyone wants anything from the village. A turtle cries: "Stout fellow, we're out of cumin, there's none in our village, but try the grocer in Courtney Walsh, and if he's shut, there's one by the church in Curtley Ambrose." Some hours later, the guest finds himself in Hoagy Carmichael, trying to buy an Ordnance Survey map. He does not succeed.

It is dark when he gets back. Everybody is in the bath, except the Alsatian. The guest needs a large one. In a hotel, he would ring a bell and a large one would instantly appear, flanked by cashews and stuffed olives. Where, though, do the turtles keep the booze? And should he just help himself? The Alsatian thinks not. The guest tries a cupboard, the Alsatian tries a bark, a turtle appears in a towel and says: "Shut up, Radar! Were you after something, old son?" He gives the guest the large tapwater he asks for, and goes out again.

Never mind. As soon as everyone has vacated the bathrooms, he will have a nice cold bath to empty, unused, and then there will be dinner. He can smell fish. Who knows, Mr Daily may well have caught a few choice gudgeon, possibly a fat frog or two. And after dinner, fifty lovely local people are coming over to the turtles' renovated barn for square-dancing to the talented Daily Trio. "Yes, Western clothes, old son, stetsons, cowboy boots, chaps, kerchiefs, usual gear. What? Oh God, didn't you get our note? How unfortunate!"

How hellish.

The departure of a weekend guest who didn't leave by four on Sunday...

Introduction

Have you, dear prospective reader, ever had so much as a passing fantasy that at the end of a weekend or fortnight your host was going to recover from the shock of your departure comparatively quickly? That he was devilish glad to be rid of you?

Did you ever have a sneaking feeling that he and his wife, partner, boyfriend, mother or whatever, might, in unison with their dogs and children, be punching the air and getting out the Bollinger before you had even rounded the corner?

Did you ever feel that during your visit you might conceivably not have been at your brilliant best for one hundred per cent of the time? Even that you might – just conceivably – tell it not in Gath – have been having an off week?

If so, do not despair. It takes years and a great deal of practice to become that prodigy – the Guest from Hell. One does not after all collect one's first "Strad" from Boosey and Hawkes on a Monday afternoon and treat those attending the Albert Hall to Beethoven's Violin Concerto on the Tuesday.

There is no such thing as a born guest – a "natch". Guesting is an art form. It takes a lifetime of practice to perfect the technique. The Guest from Hell is in reality a good guest. Every host needs a visit from the Guest from Hell. He helps hosts to pull up their socks, raise their standards and generally get their house in order.

Armed with this modest tome you will never again look back and, if you do, you will observe the stunned disbelief of those you have just left that you should, after a sojourn with them of but a few brief weeks, have deprived them of your company. You will be *persona* forever *grata*. Your run-of-the-mill untutored guest may well in his humble way stink after three days. The sweet smell of success shall continue, after you have digested these pages, to attend each occasion on which you confer upon some grateful host the privilege of your company.

And if winter should give way to spring and spring to summer and still you cannot bear to be so selfish as to remove yourself, you will be able to remain safe in the knowledge that in your case you could never ever outstay your welcome.

I give you then the good Guest from Hell. May it help you on your itinerant way.

The Guest from Hell
and the Opening Gambit

The first fallacy a guest must eradicate from his mind is that he is in some way "beholden". Such phrases as "how sweet of you to have me" must never fall from his lips. On the other hand if his hostess should say to him, "we are so thrilled you could come," he should take all steps possible to encourage such an attitude. Let him not respond half-heartedly. Let there never be the slightest element of self-deprecation. "And I am thrilled to be here too" would strike absolutely the wrong note. Much better that he simply murmurs, "I understand just how you must feel." This conveys the right message and leads them to assume that he has, out of sheer compassion for the dullness of their lives, turned down endless subsequent invitations of a much more acceptable nature. They will end up congratulating themselves on having taken the precaution of booking him up so long in advance.

It is on the very doorstep – at the point of entry – that the tone is set for the entire visit. Even perhaps in the drive. He opens the boot and stares balefully at the two enormous suitcases containing his bare necessities for the weekend. He does not actually say he has a bad back. In fact he makes it clear shortly afterwards that his back is in excellent working order. From the outset he wishes to establish a *proper working relationship,* i.e. ensure that his host, who is so fortunate to have him as a guest, does not allow him to lift a digit, let alone an entire hand.

As the host dicky-heartedly prepares to lumber up the stairs, reflecting that a few years ago if you took over 20 kilos on an air journey you were surcharged, the satanic one leaps upon the trophy wife. No peck on each cheek for him. When he eventually puts her down and gives her a moment to adjust her blouse he does go so far as to observe that the weekend could be an extremely rewarding experience. "Careful of that suitcase, old boy," he shouts up the stairs, "it's already got marks on it from your walls."

The wickedly good guest at this point follows his host to the bedroom, together with the old boy's attractive bimbo who will with any luck hold his hand on the way up, or at least wink at him.

At this stage he should continue the tone-setting process. After devoting a moment to explaining that he always takes away plenty of books etc. in case they should get flooded, which in part accounts for the weight of his luggage, he casts an eye over the room. He has made it a rule, whether in a hotel or a private house, never to accept unquestioningly the first room offered. He once asked to move operating theatres because the one in which he found himself did not face south.

"Is this your one and only spare room with an ensuite bath-room?" he enquires. "Is there a problem?" asks his host, suddenly ill at ease about the adequacy of his accommodation. The room is actually not too bad, containing as it does an emperor-size bed, whisky and biscuits. It was completely refurbished, save for the curtains, but six months previously. "Dear boy," he says with his customary diffidence, "I think I know you well enough. It's what I expect you call the drapes. Of course I realise you inherited them from the previous owners and haven't had time to put up some-thing more, how shall I say, acceptable, but I honestly don't think I'd sleep a wink in this room even with the light out. I mean, just thinking about them." Host and hostess are now totally on the run.

He, of course, knows full well, and they know he knows, that George has been in the house for nigh on thirty years and that the curtains were chosen by his previous wife. It would embarrass Cicely deeply were he to explain.

At which point with any luck Cicely will say, "Well, the bed is made up in the green room. I use it when George snores." The great joy about snoring of course is that the next day, when his

"Careful of that suitcase, old boy—it's already got marks on it from your walls..."

wife tells him he was snoring, he has no way of proving he wasn't. On being told that George is anyway on excellent nasal form he settles for the green room.

— *The Pre-emptive Strike* —

The Guest from Hell telephones well in advance to "get things straight". It saves trouble in the long run.

"I cannot tell you how much I am looking forward to visiting your gracious home." He being frugal in the extreme with his compliments, this fulsome description of their totally boring abode will quite certainly produce the hoped-for response.

"My lady wife and I await your visit with the keenest anticipation. Is there anything we can do during your all-too-brief stay with us?"

"Well, had you not asked I would not have presumed to mention it, but there is the small matter of my allergies."

"Dear fellow, fell free to tell me all. Forewarned is forearmed and all that. We may not have seen each other since the dawn of time until you button-holed me in the club, but we were, you tell me, at school together."

"Indeed. Same dorm in fact. You will therefore recall that I'll have to have pillows stuffed with goose down. Harrods used to stock them. Don't know if they still do. Try Fortnum's."

"If that's all, no problem."

"Beef medium rare with some fat. Can't bear having the *Telegraph* in the house. No poodles. *EastEnders* is a must. We can always record it if you are entertaining.

"If you were wondering about wine, I prefer Pomerol. Trotenoy, Vieux Château Certain at a pinch. Nothing to beat Petrus of course if you can run to it. I am allergic to most English cheeses and all pasteurised ones. Try jeroboams. And MCC ties. I get a migraine at the very mention of a quiche. My doctor, who is very into alternative medicine, has told me to eat as much *foi gras*

"Just to let you know before I arrive that my doctor has told me to eat as much foie gras as I can and to wash it down with a decent Sauternes..."

as I can and to wash it down with a decent Sauternes, preferably from Berry Brothers. If you are cutting back, *foie gras de canard* will do perfectly well. He is trying to put new life into my liver. I can drink any whisky except Bells or Grants. Dimple Haig and Johnny Walker Black Label agree with me best.

"I usually have my breakfast about 8am and rise at 9.30. Just knock and leave it outside. Eggs soft but cooked right through. *Times* and *Mail*. You will really hardly notice I am there. I try to fit in a snooze after lunch so if you could do your mowing and so on in the forenoon it would be a gesture in the right direction. I only wish I had green fingers.

"By the way, is your car fully insured if you leave it out? Great. Then you won't mind if I put mine in your garage. And another thing – I do hope I'm not keeping you – is laundry sent away or done in-house? Shall I leave mine outside the door each night – with my shoes, of course – then you can do what you like with it.

"I expect you will be inviting some of the locals round on Saturday evening. I could not disagree more strongly with my urban friends. I find people who live in the country absolutely fascinating – in small doses. I really have come round to your way of thinking. When they foregather at the dinner table they talk about the real issues. Hunting, farming subsidies, the village fête, septic tanks, doing up the barn, natural childbirth. Riveting stuff. Lovely to get away from the smoke and down to the nitty-gritty.

"Can't wait. Dead casual for dinner, you say. Got the picture – would I strike the right note in a Barbour? OK then, a cardie. Pip pip and give my love to you-know-who."

The "Love me, love my pooch" Guest

Charles King has a dog. His name is Phi-Phi. He is a King Charles. Charles and Phi-Phi are inseparable. Phi-Phi is various things. For instance, Phi-Phi is vociferous in a high-pitched way.

"I find people who live in the country absolutely fascinating..."

Charles never asks whether dogs are welcome or whether those he is favouring with a visit own a potential Crufts supreme champion who happens to be on heat. He and Phi-Phi just roll up. Phi-Phi moults. Phi-Phi is in fact one of life's great moulters. Hairs everywhere. Despite Phi-Phi's small size he is athletic and a great climber.

Floor to chair, chair to dining-room table: piece of cake; or more likely the eight plates of smoked salmon laid in advance as the first course. Splendid appetite.

Phi-Phi does not believe in instant intimacy. Those who religiously feed him at table over a sustained period may eventually be allowed to stroke the disposable coat that Charles so lovingly brushes on the sofa. Passing acquaintances stretching out a friendly hand in his direction are likely to find themselves *en route* for the medicine cabinet.

Phi-Phi has a weakness for curtains, particularly if there is a bitch in the house. "Dear old Phi-Phi," says Charles with that laid-back-not-to-worry attitude that puts the whole thing in perspective. "You must understand, just marking-out his territory." Phi-Phi paws affectionately at tights during dinner, but never begs. Begging is alien to Phi-Phi's nature. Demanding is not. If Phi-Phi is not fed at table, Phi-Phi gets cross. He paws, he scratches and if still ignored he has been known to nip.

Phi-Phi will, if pressed, go for a walk, or more precisely a roll. Phi-Phi has a thing about cow-pats. Unless there are any goose-droppings around. Phi-Phi sits on sofas. Particularly after he has rolled in cow-pats or goose droppings. Phi-Phi, alas, being a mere dog, cannot sign the visitors' book. There is, however, nothing to stop him leaving a calling card.

" don't worry; Woofy's only marking out his territory..."

An Ode to a Faithful Hound

Our Dobermann
Is a sober man
He hardly touches a drop.
A little sherry at lunchtime
But he knows just when to stop.
When he has been for his walkies
He likes a glass of beer,
But he never touches Advocaat
Unless he's feeling queer.
He usually has his din-din
Just after six o'clock,
And clearly finds that Winalot
Goes very well with hock.
Yes, our Dobermann is a sober man
But do not give him brandy;
The last time that he had some
He bit the postman's handy.

Will I Prick-Lightly — A Master of Etiquette on the Killing Fields

Will's host will set great store on whether he is a good shot. He may also, if he is one of life's worriers, have a passing interest in whether he is a safe shot.

A laid-back approach to the question of safety will help re-assure the host that Will is not new to the game. A playful swing through the line, producing a fully loaded gun from the car with the safety-catch off. That sort of thing. Will should, on reaching his peg, fire a couple of shots to show his host that he is in place.

Alternatively, he can carry a small hunting horn in his cartridge bag.

His host probably carries a good stock of cartridges, but Will buys a few of his own to fall back on. The best way that he can bring home to the guns on either side of him the quality of his shooting is, just as they are mounting their guns in order to shoot birds directly in front of them, to have a quick pot at them (the birds rather than the adjoining guns). In the event of success this is known as "wiping their eye". Will tries to bear in mind that someone who fails to kill a bird cleanly is known as a prick.

The normal tip for the keeper is 10p per bird shot. Thus if, say, the bag is 227 birds Will, mindful that both "over and under" tipping are equally undesirable, will carefully count out £22.70. Those unfamiliar with the decimal system should arm themselves with a pocket calculator.

Only female guns should sport over and unders, on account of their being vaguely suggestive.

Shooting guests should dress the part. Jodhpurs surviving from pig-sticking days never fail to impress. Likewise a khaki topee is most practical. Should any Belgian, French or Italian be taking part in the same shoot a bullet-proof waistcoat is *de rigueur* and full police riot gear most advisable. Germans are different. They never pepper you by accident – only when they don't like you.

Failing a topee, a feather-emblazoned Tyrolean hat worn with a tightly waisted tartan jacket looks extremely well, particularly when accompanied by a waxed moustache. Socks in Garrick club colours send an appropriate message.

On no account should the shooting guest feel obliged to remain at his peg. It is simply put there by the keeper to give him a rough idea of where he would like him to stand. Should it happen, as from time to time it is bound to do, that a decent quantity of birds are *not* obligingly flying directly over the shooting guest at an unmissable height, then he should either uproot his peg and move it to another position or, if he finds this

The 'guest from hell', on finding that a decent quantity of birds are not obligingly flying directly over him at an unmissable height – uproots his peg and moves it to a more advantageous position....

burdensome, simply stroll amiably in the direction of he who happens to be occupying what is known as the "hot spot".

This fortunate fellow may be wearing cans (ear defenders to the non-shooting proletariat). Our guest therefore shouts. This will make his colleague jump and miss, whereupon our hero calmly dispatches the bird. His shout should also have caused what is known as a flush. This does not mean that the gun he has just addressed has gone purple with rage. It does mean that endless waves of birds, reminiscent of the attack on Pearl Harbor, are now flying over both of them. With a jocular "Plenty of work for two here," he proceeds to stand shoulder to shoulder. Being in such close proximity he announces, "Mine, I think," every time his colleague raises his gun to his shoulder.

The shooting guest is the proud owner of an overweight minia-ture schnauzer named Humphrey. This improbable beast has absorbed, from watching the spaniels and labradors, a few rudi-mentary notions about retrieving. Being completely untrained he nevertheless watches birds fall, marks them and, having a particu-larly good nose, frequently finds birds in the undergrowth while the extremely expensive graduates of gun-dog finishing schools are wandering aimlessly around. If a neighbour has, in Humphrey's opinion, too impressive a pile of birds beside him then Humphrey will consider it his duty and pleasure to redress the balance. If things get boring he occupies himself making the birds oven-ready. He does everything but tie the bacon round.

It is over drinks before lunch that the men are sorted out from the boys. The shooting guest has his answers ready. "Lost count. Forty or so. That's on the first drive, of course. Mainly rights and lefts. Stratospheric."

To an ashen-faced gun. "Damned good shot. I saw it. Pity it was a white one. Our hostess's pet over three seasons I am told. Not to worry. All's fair in love and war. Doubtless you failed to hear the keeper begging us on no account to ... I say, Delia seems to be in tears. You had better go and cheer her up. How about singing 'I'm longing for a white pheasant' to her?"

⚊ *The Antique Dealer Guest from Hell* ⚊

From time to time it happens that some humble owner of a country house and contents is gratified and honoured to receive a visit from a purveyor of antiques. "Angela, I have some splendid news," our much-chuffed homesteader will intone to his down-trodden wife, whose spouse lives it up in London all week with various other women while she milks yak, mucks out the stables and buffs up the furniture with Mr Sheen. "Yes, splendid indeed, Cecil Sneerworthy is tearing himself away from his commodious gallery in Mount Street and will, together with his partner Charles Heppledale, be with us this very evening."

Angela and Fred hurl themselves into a positive frenzy of activity. By the time their guests arrive there is not an Aubusson un-Hoovered, nor an un-Windowleened Lowry. At the appointed hour two beautiful people emerge from a mauve Range Rover and greet Angela in those careful voices reserved for those who owe their accents to elocution lessons.

"How do you do," enunciates Cecil carefully. Angela confidently expects him to tell her that in Hertfordshire, Herefordshire and Hampshire hurricanes hardly ever hoccur. Instead of which he gazes around their hall. This phases Angela not, for Fred has explained that they are probably wildly underinsured and he'd rather push out the boat on the Mouton Rothschild than pay them an exorbitant fee.

This happens to Cecil and Charles just about every time they manage to fix themselves up with a free weekend out of town. It creates a number of tricky but not insoluble problems. What should the antique dealer Guest from Hell do when he is shown a pair of commodes that turn out to be priceless but not in the way that his host and hostess have until that moment supposed?

Let us eavesdrop on Cecil as he encounters just this situation. "I see," says Fred, "you have not failed to notice the commodes on either side of the fireplace which is, by the way, considered to be the work of Grinling Gibbons. The fireplace, not the commodes."

"Pull the other one," Cecil murmurs before he can check himself. Fred obediently tugs at one of the commodes thereby displaying a back that is both brand new and also contemporary with the rest of it.

Cecil first says probingly that he is sure these commodes recently came up at auction. If Fred says, "Right in one, I successfully bid for them at Sotheby's," then the matter is much simplified.

"Within the last five years I trust?" enquires Cecil (that being the limit of Sotheby's guarantee). So long as they were bought in a major saleroom and so long as Fearless Fred was immodest enough to have bid for them himself, Cecil may without compunction and even with a degree of relief tell Fred the unvarnished truth.

But supposing Fred says, "No, I bought them from a highly reputable Bond Street dealer some time ago". Then Cecil might well have to be more circumspect. Were he to titter gracefully and suggest that a highly reputable Bond Street dealer was an oxymoron he might undermine that confidence in the British antiques trade which is so vital to its dominant position in the world market. There is of course Malletts. Perhaps the most ravishing antiques shop in England. The epitome of elegance. The soul of probity. But then – every rule must have an exception.

Anyway, in that event Cecil must walk a tightrope. "I think your commodes are ravishing – in fact they need the fullest possible documentation. Now the BADA at Rutland Gate runs an arbitration service. I would take full advantage of this facility and you will then have your commodes studied in depth by a panel of experts who will report back to you having first researched them. Provenance is vital, you know." This should pass the buck just nicely.

Fred, of course, might have said, "I bought them from the Den of Antiquity in Brighton a few days ago," in which case, the Den of Antiquity being Cecil and Charles's most deadly rival and a damned nuisance in the auction rooms, Cecil may safely let fly. "Firewood," he may intone. "Charles, do you not agree? Brand spanking new. I trust your cheque has not yet cleared. I do think, Fred, if I may so address you (it behoves even the grandest trades-man to show a modicum of diffidence; customers love it), if you must swim in dangerous seas you should draw the line at piranha-infested waters such as Brighton."

The commodes having been dealt with one way or another Cecil and Charles will then make suitably appreciative noises at any possession of their host and hostess that appears on casual inspection to be at least in part genuine.

As they proceed around the house our two entrepreneurs will bear their current inventory very much in mind. The merest sus-picion of a gap will bring them up short as a Dartmoor haircut. One will grab the other's arm and stare at the space in stupefied disbelief, indicating what a tragedy is such a gaping void, nay it is even a sin, that being blessed with such a gracious home they see fit to leave this corner or that corridor, or both, unloved.

In no time at all they have described in glowing terms the fruit-wood free-standing corner cupboard with original butterfly hinges and the "divine" miniature oak settle (so useful if you want to break your journey on the way to the bedroom). By a happy coincidence Cecil has to pass their very door on Monday in his mauve Volvo (the Range Rover only appears at weekends) and it will be no trouble at all to drop them off.

In view of their generous hospitality Charles hardly likes to mention the price, but he steels himself to the task. Fred and Angela are suitably impressed. Cecil and Charles will, for they

"This gaping void is just screaming out for this divine miniature oak settle
I have in stock – so useful for breaking the journey between the bedroom and bathroom..."

are much practised at the art, sidle admiringly through the entire weekend without putting an exact figure on any object whatsoever.

As they make their getaway, having eaten like queens and drunk like lords, both at home and in the nearby Relais rip-off, they thank Angela and Fred warmly, warn them they are no doubt grossly underinsured and Charles would be only too happy to visit them in a professional capacity (£200 plus VAT per hour plus travel, typist etc.).

The Prepared-for-anything Guest

Flashy Featherlight was not a boy scout for nothing. He keeps the movement's motto ever in mind. He is at all times ready and willing to perform any service that may be required of him. To that end he will pack a separate suitcase, the key to which he will not hand over to the butler. Whereas some gentlemen's gentlemen will lay out handcuffs, strait-jacket, ball gags, hoods etc. with total equanimity, others are wont to become over-excited.

Flashy, belying his name, is the soul of discretion and tends to wait for she-who-may-be-in-need to make the first move. Mind you, should his napkin fall from his knee and should his neighbour at the time be allowing her tongue to run playfully along her upper set, then he may venture to run his own equally playfully up her right calf while retrieving the old double damask.

Any female of biddable age (16–78) leaving her bedroom door unlocked at night would be insulted if Flashy were not to arrive only in his bathrobe, suitcase in hand, with an offer of assistance. Were she to go so far as to tip-toe across the passage to the loo, Flashy would construe such a move as a positive *cri de coeur*. He would be upon her in a (and I use the phrase advisedly) flash.

Those females in holy orders or on parole from convents have invariably been found by Flashy to be particularly grateful for a

"Your things are all laid out, Sir – including your handcuffs..."

little "how is your Father?" Such females are quite frequently given, in fact, to murmuring afterwards, "Father, forgive me but thanks a bundle."

Foreplay can take many forms – a spin on Flashy's Harley Davidson for instance. Half an hour riding pillion and some girls are anyone's. A couple of Martinis as she skips out of her leathers – or not as the case might be – and Robert is your mother's brother. With the Joan Hunter Dunns, but not alas, the Virginia Wades of this world, an ace is worth two finesses, i.e. the guest's service on the court, if good enough, may well lead to another service being rendered off it.

A walk through the woods – sheltering from a sudden shower in the summer house – a punt up a leafy stream, Flashy looking his absolute best in panama with Hawkes club hatband and pale blue blazer (both borrowed from some muscle-bound acquaintance). Hiding in a wardrobe during a jolly game of sardines. The possibilities are interminable. Flashy, devoid of one selfish fibre in his whole body, will endeavour to provide a memorable weekend for any attractive female whom he feels could do with an hour or two of remedial exercise.

This commendable unselfishness is in no way confined to his own personal activities. There are limits to what one chap can do. He therefore regards it as his mission to decide who is or should be mad for whom and then proceeds to promote total togetherness within the available time-span.

He gets told *she* is the Princess Easy-Lay of Hampstead and loaded to the gunwales. *She* gets told *he*, despite the fact that his surname is Jones, is positively transfused with Latin blood and that those many females who expire after dallying with him announce with their terminal breath that it was worth it.

When *she* then finds a red rose on her pillow, together with a note that Keith Jones sends his best wishes, nature must take its course, lust will find a way and passions will be requited. Particularly as Flashy has left a note from *her* to *him* on *his* pillow identifying her bedroom and stipulating a time.

Needless to say Flashy is always ready to lend any form of equipment that may be needed.

His deep and abiding interest in the welfare of his fellow guests makes it necessary for him to keep himself as fully informed as possible. Should he mistakenly assume A was getting on frightfully well with B and C with D, whereas in fact A was getting on famously with D or even C, then disaster can loom. To avoid any possibility of misconception, or to be more precise of miscopulation, Flashy will perforce sacrifice his slumber in order to wait, door ajar, his eye fixed unblinkingly on the landing.

By the end of the night, armed with a complete log of each guest's nocturnal perambulations, he is in a very strong position.

Not a creaking floorboard, not the twang of a sprung mattress, but it is recorded.

This omniscience can yield dividends. When Q realises that Flashy is aware that she has conferred favours on W, she may well come to the conclusion that there is only one way to ensure Flashy's absolute discretion on the matter and that is to compromise him too.

The Barrister and the Archdeacon

The barrister guest Simon receives innumerable invitations to break bread at top tables. This is due in large measure to his being an unencumbered male.

When Simon gave Archdeacon Hallelujah and his church mouse of a spouse a bell, or if you prefer it, got on the blower to accept their kind offer of an evening meal, the Archdeacon was less than plussed when, just before the end of their conversation, Simon let slip that he would be accompanied by his latest pièce de crackling, Grace.

Had the church mouse been the one to pick up the receiver, and had Simon merely enquired as to whether bringing Grace along was a good idea, Mrs Hallelujah would have said that much as she and the venerable one would have liked to meet his new girlfriend, who was doubtless a tribute to his flawless taste in companions, a joy to behold, the embodiment of piety and a treasure chest of inspiring mealtime conversation, it would throw the numbers out and it would be a pleasure to entertain her on some future occasion.

When Hezekiah (being the Christian name of this Christian fellow) explained to Minnie that Simon had disposed rather than proposed she came perilously close to muttering some such obscenity as "Oh, bother" under her breath. With a sigh the placement was returned to the drawing board.

As they had no time that week to go to Habitat to buy a bigger table, they had to content themselves with trying to enlist the help of Hezekiah's employer by praying that one of the female guests would go down with something not too serious. Their supplications were ignored.

The great day dusked.

The guests were invited for 8pm. Not wishing to see their priestly host wrapped in a shroud and his pet rodent wearing a crown of Carmen curlers they took the seaman-like precaution of arriving a few minutes after the appointed hour. All, that is, except Simon and Grace, who arrived many minutes after the appointed hour. By 9pm Minnie had decided to rechristen the cheese soufflés. "Pancakes" would do nicely, she thought.

At 9.15pm she threw them down the sink and knocked up her *tiède pamplemousse* – a last minute Godsend – and ushered the incomplete assembly in to dine.

At 9.40pm, while Hezekiah was attacking a *gigot d'agneau* which, earlier in the evening, had been a pleasing shade of pink, with a venom brought about by someone having mentioned female priests, the door bell rang. There, poised on the "Welcome in the name of God" mat, was the imperturbable Simon. "Ah, ah" said the Archdeacon and waited. The stopped watch routine? A rush to judge's lodgings to seek an injunction?

Simon merely beamed with pride and waved in the direction of the thing in shades that drooped beside him clutching flowers. Rather nice flowers actually. It takes little to assuage a man of the cloth. He is ever-conscious of the divinity of forgiveness.

"You must be Grace," he intoned in that jolly voice he normally reserved for reading the banns. "I suppose," she said after a pause, "I must be. What a perceptive little chap you are," adding in her particularly unattractive, adenoidal drawl, "would you put these in water – until we leave?"

Hezekiah returned to the candlelit room. Grace, still in her Raybans, she being a first-time caller, was placed on her host's right-hand side, while on her right sat a somewhat deaf, retired Brigadier with lovely manners, sporting a moustache. "This is Grace," announced the Archdeacon. The party rose to their feet and bowed their heads.

The genial old buffer in the Gunner tie kicked off with his usual ice-breaker, "Have you – ah – harrumph – come far?" Grace looked him up and down with infinite disdain, dropped her ash on his *gigot d'agneau* and drawled, "Just how small do you like your talk?" He beamed. "You say you decided to walk. That no doubt is what kept you."

"What …" continued the Brigadier with his time-honoured supplementary, "do you – ah – what ho – do?" She looked at him pityingly. "I am self-employed. That is to say I mind my own business."

Simon lent across the table and blew her a kiss. "Grace," he announced with unalloyed pride, "is a feminist," at which point she stubbed out her cigarette in the butter dish.

"Bully for her," bellowed the Brigadier, "there are far too many of these damned lesbians around."

"You are the absolute pits," she gave him as scathing a look as one can when one's eyes are blacked out. The Brigadier adjusted his hearing aid and decided she had told him he was an absolute hit. He leant forward. "Tell me, my dear Grace, those sunglasses, touch of conjunctivitis, eh? Better soon, I trust."

That was it. She bared her capped teeth at him and snarled. She rushed from the room and moments later stood in the doorway clutching her flowers. She slammed the front door as she fled. The rest, happily including Simon, stayed on to enjoy the Archdeacon's favourite Pomerol, Château L'Eglise.

The Archdeacon felt a few words were called for on the subject of the newly departed. "Grace …" he began. The party rose to their feet and bowed their heads.

PS. Simon, mind you, sometimes takes with him to a party not just one passing fancy but several. Ideally he is invited to one of

those informal dos that take place around Christmas for neighbours. "Do bring any family or friends that you happen to have
with you."

Simon sees that as a convenient and economical way of throwing a cocktail party for his many lovely acquaintances, in someone
else's house. He rings up everyone he wants to work off. "My
place around a quarter to twelve – a quick glass *chez moi* – and
then Freddie, who lives hard by, and I are laying on a combined
thrash." They are not of course. Freddie will be totally appalled as
Simon ushers in thirty of his less-speakable cronies.

The "I think I know you well enough" Guest

It is often said that the good host and hostess should *de temps en
temps* decamp to each of their guest rooms.

Some do. Some do not. In fact there are houses to which our
guest-from-you-know-where is bidden which convey the impression that the owners have long since lost their hearing, their sight,
their sense of smell and their taste, in both senses of the word.
They treat dust as though it were some glorious patina that must
on no account be disturbed. So oblivious are they to the gurgling
of the pipes, the creak of floorboards, the melodious chiming of
their Tompion at fifteen-minute intervals throughout the night,
that they are clearly taking unfair advantage of the peace they
enjoy when, having turned in, they remove their deaf-aids. As for
their olfactory organs ... Be it incontinent cats, dead rats under
the floorboards, drains or rotting food in the larder, the amazing
thing is that the host and hostess are for one reason or another
totally impervious to – in fact almost seem to relish – such
odours. "Ah, lovely to be home," they say to each other as they
breast the domestic porch and take a deep sniff.

" How curious - I've never before seen dust treated,
as some glorious patina not to be disturbed..."

Even the very decorations themselves can, on occasions, only have been designed to cause suffering to their visitors. Our guest once counted seventeen different patterns, all busy, in his modest-sized bedroom. He would far rather, being an aesthetic soul, have passed the weekend in either the Chamber of Horrors or Bedlam.

He, having devoted much of his adult life to living in other people's houses, is only too familiar with the problems touched upon above. He realises that countless others before him have stoically endured the filth, the stench and the cacophony that characterise your average English country house, without breathing a word to Bessie, Cynthia, Mabel or whoever.

Our guest is, however, made of sterner stuff that the uncomplaining wimps who have preceded him. He has about him a missionary zeal – an inbuilt urge – to bring the homes of those he is so public-spirited as to visit, up to snuff.

"I think I know you well enough," prefaces every criticism. He continues, "to tell you that there is no lavatory brush in my bathroom, that my bath water was tepid, my towel on the small side and the bed so uncomfortable that both my Tibetan spaniel and I gave it up as a bad job and slept on the floor." His host and hostess are, of course, immensely grateful to be told.

Many guests keep their own counsel, but any shortcomings are best brought out into the open by a friendly word or two. Some, however, are most successfully and subtly indicated by the use of apparatus. The donning by our hero of the type of gauze mask much used by urban cyclists, whenever he must enter the larder, may well encourage those sheltering him to ask themselves whether he is doing this for a reason. In similar vein, he may also appear downstairs in order to take the newspaper his host was about to read up to his bedroom, still wearing his dressing gown and the shooting socks in which he passed the night.

As to cleanliness, he always brings an apron with him, clad in which he enquires where they keep their Hoover, duster, wax polish, razor blade for scraping the rust off the bath etc. An hour or two in his bedroom whirring away and then he asks for a bucket of water. "Shan't be long, just going to wash down the woodwork." By the time he moves in on the drawing room or whatever they call it, and enlists the help of his fellow guests, he invariably finds that he is beginning to get his message across.

The sun is now over what his host, who is engaged on an endless search for a sense of humour, laughingly refers to as the metre-arm. Drinks are forthcoming. "As we were in the same dorm at school I am going to take courage. This tonic is as flat as a pancake and the crisps belie their name. And Angela, my dear, you have a ladder in your tights and your dress is coming apart at the back. You don't mind my telling you, do you?"

There are those who take the view that when one's host has made a total codswallop of the meal it is more tactful to gloss over the matter. Old Nick's sidekick is not one of them. "My dear Cynthia. This is not just provençal, it is positively rustic," he will chirp merrily. "Is this grouse or liver?" rarely fails to get a reaction from a hostess who had had such a struggle squeezing into her dress that she forgot to switch on the oven. "Don't tell me, it's chicken tartare à la salmonella," he cries, "do you happen to have a microwave?"

⚊ *Charles Croesus and the Much-blessed* ⚊

Charles does not inflict himself upon paupers. The ill-to-do have quite enough to contend with and he hates having to say no. He is sure they would make every effort to repay. He does understand how much she must want to attend her mother's funeral in Rio de Janeiro. Such a bright boy should certainly take up his place at Oxford. If Harold could only have it done privately they might well catch it in time.

He is much too soft-hearted to dare expose himself to such

"Is this grouse or liver?..."

heart-bypassing pleas. Also, were he to put at risk even the tiniest fraction of the considerable portfolio of shares left to him by his uncle Ebenezer it would be a breach of trust. The old boy's ashes would turn in their urn. If there was one thing the old chap could not tolerate it was a good cause.

On the other hand there is no limit to the degree of wealth that our fearless freebie-hunter is prepared to tolerate. Lesser men might, on coming across nineteen shimmering Aston Martins taking up all the available space in Wilton Crescent, the property of a man whose *pied-à-terre* was worth a cool ten big ones, be so consumed with envy as to be inhibited from giving of their best.

Charles envies such men not.

He knows that the five hundred richest men in the country are also the five hundred unhappiest. They are obsessed with the temporary nature of their solvency. They are totally preoccupied with their mortality. Most of them are convinced that the hospital to which they have donated millions has failed to show its gratitude by diagnosing the various terminal diseases from which they are quite definitely suffering. Furthermore, the financial markets are involved in a conspiracy with the sole object of removing their hard-earned few pennies. Their stockbrokers hate them and should have sold in time. Indeed, their failure to do so is almost criminal. They should have known their client's wishes. The fact that their client, due to the fact that because he was shooting six days a week/fishing all season/skiing half the winter/spending spring on a yacht in the West Indies, never actually got around to contacting said poor bloody broker has absolutely nothing to do with it.

One or two of the top five hundred are mean. Pay telephones in the hall. Condom machines in the loos. All breakages charged for. Charles gives this particular breed a wide berth. By and large the ultra mega-rich make reasonably free with their dosh. The mistress will be housed in comfort even if the surroundings ensure privacy by being somewhat less than central. Her earrings will come from Tiffany's because her benefactor has simply never heard of Ken Lane. As for those invited to visit his network of off-shore-owned houses, they do tend by and large to be almost as revoltingly rich as him, but not quite. He does not like to be out-mega-bucked. From time to time he will introduce into the midst the token pauper, who may even be Old Labour to boot. His job will be to go round the house frowning at the priceless knick-knacks. He has, mind you, to mind his tongue. His host did not receive his knighthood solely on account of his lavish donations to the Conservative party. No, no. He also saved various museums from insolvency and even endowed a chair at a university, notwithstanding that he was too thick to get into one himself.

It therefore ill behoves the token pauper to point out that each Lowry on display would feed a starving infant in a developing country until said infant was old enough to rape and pillage for himself.

Occasionally the blessed guest is chosen as the token pauper and summoned for a weekend where he will discover "beyond the dreams of avarice" to be the ultimate oxymoron.

The dream never dies. To own the second-best grouse moor or the second-biggest yacht is not enough. Paranoia is never far away. What are they saying of him in the club? The final insult – that he is a nice enough chap but keeps rather a low profile? That he does not know how to spend his money? Soon the trusty old Merc with the two telephones and the fax is discreetly advertised in *Exchange & Mart* along with the Canaletto that turned out to be "school of". To hell with it. He will throw discretion to the winds. If Michael Winner can have an open-topped Rolls, so can he. What should Charles take such a man when he is bidden?

Flowers? Hardly; he has a private army of gardeners. He has orchids coming out of his ears and sunflowers shine out of his you-know-what.

Charbonnel and Walker chocolates? Diabetes, cholesterol. What are you trying to do to him? You know his life hangs by a thread.

He usually settles for a subscription to *Private Eye*. People love to read about themselves.

And how should he behave? Should he fawn? Or should he pull him down a peg or two? In a word "yes". E.g. "Your shares are doing incredibly well. Despite that outrageous piece in the *FT*. I can never understand why people go on about gearing." "You really are looking fit. As did your father until the very day he died. He must have been just about your age. Wonderful way to go. Just after he landed it. When are you off again? Next week, eh. Tight lines and don't overdo it." "Cracking champagne. Used to be my favourite. Until they were taken over."

Charles does find one visit to such OTT establishments to be quite enough. You never know when these chaps are giving you a red-hot insider-trading tip or when they are trying to push up the price of one of their ailing companies. They did not, after all, get where they are today by being soft as butter ...

No, by and large, once is enough. Well, maybe once a year. Just often enough to remind oneself how awful it must be to have so much money.

— *A Visit to the Nouveaux Pauvres* —

In the old days Francis Furlonger used to be bidden to the Bullingham-Manners on properly engraved cards. None of your laser rubbish. Seven thirty for eight. Black tie. RSVP. If the guest list was impressive it was enclosed. The door would be opened by a butler. Courtesy of Searcy's. The Dom Perignon was shrouded in damask but its particular shape still identified it.

If no one was sensitive enough to comment on the wine, Charles himself worked the conversation round to it with hardly a whiff of subtlety. "The 61s are holding up very well," he would murmur, holding his Dartington against the beeswax to show off the deep purple, "particularly (if applicable) the first growths."

The château we had to guess. This was not a formidable challenge if you had taken the precaution of discovering which was the most expensive and fashionable château and vintage of the moment. You also had to take into consideration the calibre of those round the table, e.g. Chairman of ICI, go for Petrus; someone from Lazards, Bechevelle; someone from the Min. of Ag. and Fish., go for something Icelandic. Carriages at 11.30pm. Charles was inevitably up early the next morning commuting over to the Big Apple to become even richer and needed his full quota of shut-eye.

All that was before the recession. Francis had a telephone call from Miriam the other day inviting him to kitchen supper. "Very casual," she trilled. "Come as you are. No need to wear a tie."

The door was opened by Tantalus their son. He, poor boy, had been named for another era as had his sister Perciflage who in due course was to serve and wash up. The Bullingham-Manners, when they had christened their offspring, had failed to envisage that the time would come when Oxbridge graduates would compete vigorously for even the most humdrum of jobs and the possession of such soubriquets would not, in such a cut-throat market, enhance their prospects of employment.

No matter that their intimates knew them as Tan and Percy. Nicknames play no part in cvs. Tantalus having ushered Francis into what Miriam had always referred to as the salon, the first thing he noticed was the absence of their erstwhile pride and joy, the Lowrys. Charles at once took on board the fact that his guest was sadly but sympathetically eyeing their replacements – a motley collection of prints. "We came to the conclusion that Lowry had shot his bolt," he announced, "and decided to cash in before the bottom fell out of the market."

"Ah yes."

Charles had also been hit by Lloyd's rather hard and where it hurts most – in the bread basket. As if Outhwaite was not enough, Charles's city activities were, in the aftermath of the recession, within the merest ace of going down the proverbial plughole. Tantalus appeared with a bottle. "Dad is just mad about this stuff," he beamed, "says it knocks spots off champers. Lauderdale Ridge. It's an Aussie sparkling Chardonnay." Miriam, positively festooned in Ken Lane, ushered us down to the kitchen.

"Charles and I are breaking new ground this year," Miriam chirped as the party tucked into chilli con carne. "We are staying with friends in Guernsey." When they said they were off there in August Francis fiendishly asked whether that would not interfere with their efforts to kill and maim grouse. "I am proud to say," Miriam beamed, "that Charles has taken agin blood sports. After all, as he says to himself, our feathered friends wish us no harm, so why ...?"

She was interrupted by Charles inveighing against Rolls-Royces. "Hondas are light years ahead. Wonderful engineering. No comparison. Hold the road like limpets. Have some more claret. How does it grab you? The Bulgarians are really turning out some first-rate stuff."

Charles felt for his half-hunter, for a moment forgetting that he preferred nowadays to rely upon the digital watch he had come upon in a *Sunday Express* colour supplement. "Almost 11.30," he announced, "must call it a day. Off across the pond to the Isle of Wight tomorrow." *Plus ça change ...*

Julian Hugely-Caring and his Work for Charity

Julian has nothing against charities. He considers the Distressed Gentlefolk's Association a thoroughly worthy cause, and should he in the fullness of time get through his family's, his partner's and his own money, he would not hesitate to get in touch with them.

He is broadly in favour of the NSPCC, subject to such excellent dicta as "spare the rod and spoil the child" and "small children should be seen and not heard". He to some extent tolerates the RSPCA, although,

> *The more you beat them the better they be,*
> *A woman, a dog and a walnut tree.*

He always considered this sound sense, with the possible exception of the walnut tree.

In the meantime he receives each week more invitations to charitable events than he has consumed cold suppers. These divide neatly into two categories. "Biffy and I have taken a table at the Mansion House on the 14th of Bla two thousand and Bla when Bla Bla Bla will be singing in aid of Bla Bla Bla. We would be thrilled if you would come as our Bla Bla Bla.

A freebie. A bloodless outing. Bung Ho. It being even more blessed to receive than to give, Julian accepts with alacrity. Charity may begin at home but it also extends effortlessly to an evening out.

He has such events down to the finest of all possible arts, i.e. he keeps rolls of raffle tickets in every conceivable colour in his DJ pocket, and invariably manages to have the real winner ejected unceremoniously by the toast-master.

He also takes the tombola extremely seriously, arriving at the earliest possible moment clutching a wad of stickies. He has long since sussed out that after the first hour the indescribable sub-Charlotte's Ball Sloanes, who, to coin a phrase, man this event, ruthlessly add more blanks, thereby cutting the odds. He therefore wastes no time. Any unwanted superfluous object acquired, such as boxing gloves or a child's bicycle, can be effortlessly unloaded (at a profit) on some drunken, doting father as he sways his way out of Grosvenor House, the Mansion House or whatever, at the end of the proceedings.

If said father happens to be knee-high to a wasp he might find the latter useful for commuting from Chester Square to the City.

The more you beat them, the better they be—
a woman, a dog and a walnut tree...

Julian is keenest of all on the "Dinner for Two" lucky-dip. Being an old stager he is well aware that two thirds of the envelopes contain £5 vouchers for McDonald's. Even supposing that he can bear the thought of crossing such a threshold, choosing such an envelope entails taking a £15 loss on a £20 investment, which would never do. Such vouchers, being printed on card, are distinctly thicker than the sheet of paper on which is written "Dinner for Two at Tante Claire with wine". A surreptitious feel inside the bran tub works wonders.

The "Silent Auction", where you write your programme number alongside your bid, he also has under total control. His technique is to hold his horses until seconds before the deadline – usually 8pm. He then walks smartly along the goods on offer. Holiday for two in Benidorm value £800 has really got them going. A fight to the death between programme 109 and programme 69 has resulted in a final bid of £4,250. On the other hand "gold bracelet value £1,200" has not excited any serious interest. Some mean bugger is about to get way with a bid of £220. He is to be seen smirking nearby. Can't have that. As eight strikes the good charity guest writes in £220.50. Most satisfying. It would never do to condone mean buggery.

Occasionally the invitation comes not from some splendid, over-endowed "I'll get a knighthood whatever it costs" do-gooder offering to defray the expense of our hero's evening out, but from some aggressive skinflint trying to deprive him of what can only be described as serious money. Such unspeakable bounders usually send an enticing invitation, the joy of which becomes distinctly alloyed when the recipient turns to page two, whereon is printed "I will be happy to purchase ... tickets @ £250 each *or* I regret I cannot attend the Legover Ball in aid of superannuated indigent prostitutes but enclose my cheque made out to Lord Lay of Soho in the sum of £ ...".

It is then that Julian has one of his attacks of high-mindedness. "Dear Mr Warren," he writes, "Loath as I am not to support the charity to which you have over the years devoted so much of your energy and the committee which your good lady Mrs Warren so ably chairs, it may surprise you to learn that picking up fallen women has never been one of my recreational activities. I shall therefore not be joining you. Nevertheless, have a ball."

Other invitations call for other stratagems. "I am most honoured by your suggestion that I join you at the splendid event you are organising in aid of Macmillan Cancer Relief, the Aids Hospice, Children in Need, the National Trust, the Lifeboats, or whatever as applicable, but I have to tell you that as a Christian Scientist I find myself unable to support your worthy cause. Personally I shall be holding a soirée in aid of my faith on the first of May, tickets £250 made out to me personally, discount for cash. There will be a laying on of hands (my hands on your wallet), and demonstration of faith-healing (my faith that you will heal the wounds inflicted on me by my stockbroker).

"Do come and hear about Christian Science and how it can help you. Think of it, no more BUPA subscriptions, no private medicine, no more expensive antibiotics. These savings should enable you to contribute generously to our dinner-for-two lucky dip. I trust you are not allergic to McDonald's."

Not all appeals to his warm generous nature are related to the sick. The other day Julian was approached by one of his many benefactors.

"Dear Bill," he replied, "I cannot begin to tell you how deeply distressing I find it not to support, even in small measure, a cause as worthy as Shelter, although I have to say I simply do not understand why the homeless do not stay with friends or in a hotel until they have found suitable permanent accommodation. Please do not think I am not deeply sensitive to these poor people's problems. Why do not the banks provide bridging loans at more modest rates? I must however harden my heart, even though the appeal comes from you. Your lavish hospitality over the years has meant a great deal to me. It will not surprise you to learn – no one

knows my warm outgoing nature better than your good self —
how I scrimp and save (only the other day I jumped on board a bus
to go to St James's, notwithstanding that there was a taxi within
call) in order to contribute to worthy causes other than myself.
After deep consideration of where my discretionary income, i.e.
my few spare pennies, can do most good I decided some time ago
to concentrate on the Donkey Sanctuary in Devon. I have mislaid
the s.a.e. I am sure you kindly enclosed so I am sending you this
reply at my own expense. Yours ever, J."

The arm of coincidence, otherwise known as sod's law, being
what it is, he opened his mail the very next day only to discover a
request for money from the Donkey Sanctuary, forwarded to him
by his widowed, elder, childless sister in Guernsey. He wrote to
her at once.

"My dear Audrey,

"How splendid to hear from you. I cannot tell you how deeply
distressing I find it not to support ... decided to concentrate on
Shelter — one is, is not one, so fortunate to have a roof over one's
head?

"Pip pip,

"Your devoted younger brother.

"PS. I do hope you are in no danger of marrying that gold-digging
bounder you were telling me about."

Generally Julian extols the virtues of standing on one's own
two feet (particularly if contacted by BLESMA), planning one's
affairs in a far-sighted manner (ditto the RNIB), self-reliance
(lone parents), single-mindedness (schizophrenics), not keeping
parrots, contraception, euthanasia for others, and putting all
surplus foreign coins in the collection.

As for sponsored walks. If someone is consumed with a desire to go on a thoroughly healthy holiday in Nepal or Morocco he is only too happy to send them something – his best wishes or maybe a get-well-soon card.

The Late Guest

Tom Tardy, on being invited out to dinner, will make every effort to be on time. He always makes every effort.

Let us, however, imagine the scenario where Tom has been unavoidably delayed by an interesting programme on the television, or the crossword.

The invitation stipulates 8pm. It is by now 8.40pm. His host's house is twenty minutes away by mini-cab, which will take ten minutes to arrive. Taking his own car is out of the question as he intends to imbibe with that particular ferocity he reserves for other people's alcohol. Luckily he is not, by and large, an abusive drunk. Amorous, opinionated, somnolent, yes. Abusive only if someone disagrees with him.

Anyway, he knows he will, if all goes well, be hitting his host's door bell around 9.10pm. Should he ring with a cheery "Hold your soufflé, the Mounties are on the way"?

In a word, no. The guest who telephones to warn his host he will be late is placing himself at a grave psychological disadvantage. The host has long planned two tables of bridge. An *aide-mémoire* has been mailed to each guest. If our friend does not show, the whole evening will be ruined. Much too late now to find a bridge-playing substitute. Approximately every thirty seconds the host consults his watch and prays. All he wants is to see – however late – the cheery countenance of Tom framed in the doorway. At 8.45pm he can contain himself no longer and dials his number – only to be greeted by the answerphone.

By 9pm he is on Valium. Does he usher the six of them (seven

THE GUEST FROM HELL...

...imbibes with a particular ferocity reserved for other peoples alcohol...

counting him) in the direction of the totally ruined dinner? What can they salvage from the wreckage of the evening? One table of bridge, one of cribbage and one of patience?

At 9.10pm he hears a sound that brings tears of joy to his eyes. It is the front door bell. Tom has made it. What a terrific chap he is. What a welcome is accorded him. The Prodigal Son. For him the champagne. For the rest Blue Nun. He is not languishing in hospital. There is no need to report him missing. He lives. He is with them.

The party waits with bated breath for an account of the dramas that have befallen him and which he has so brilliantly overcome in order to be with them. He is the hero of the evening.

Now, just suppose that Tom had concluded that it would be generally thoughtful and sensitive to telephone his host and fore-warn him that he fully intended to be a teeny-weeny-bit-to-wit-seventy-minutes late, but would ultimately grace their boring gathering? He would doubtless take the opportunity to hint that his host's wife is such an appalling cook that an extra seventy minutes in the oven would be most unlikely to have any discernible effect for better or worse upon the gastronomic ghastliness – the so-called *daube de Provence* – that she has concocted.

The host replaces the receiver and breaks the news to his wife and the five guests who have sacrificed all to be on time. Daphne looks daggers at Derek who had told her as she took forty minutes to put on her face that she was wasting time trying to make a silk purse out of a sow's ear.

Charles has torn home from the office leaving important busi-ness unfinished – to be precise, prising himself from the loins of his personal and personable assistant Beverly a moment too soon. And so on . . .

All are incensed and no wonder. This unspeakable blackguard has not met with some fearful injury – he is in perfect order. He has merely chosen not to join them until 9.10pm and has actually rung up to brag about it. It is all very well for him, of course. At this very moment he is probably wallowing in Badedas, listening to Classic FM, playing with a plastic duck and saying to himself, "As I have been good enough to warn them of my late arrival there is now no need to get a move on."

Nine ten. Ten past nine. How in God's name, they ask themselves, will they last out? Is he trying to give them all duodenal ulcers? They will just have to do some serious drinking. They conclude that at 9.10pm he will doubtless turn up stone cold sober and later take a fortune off them at the table.

A campaign of hate and resentment gets underway. The tension soon mounts. "Damn poor show, these fellows who blithely get on the blower and announce that they won't be turning up until it's almost time to go. I suggest that when this bounder finally condescends to join us we should all make our feelings perfectly clear."

Percival Cockburn, whose career seems to have consisted in being a member of White's, announces that the late arrival should be horse-whipped and have his hands cut off to stop him making any more obscene telephone calls of this nature.

All in all Tom scores absolutely no Brownie points for wising-up his host in advance that he is about to kick him in the teeth.

If you are about to have it off with the neighbour's wife or daughter you do not tell your wife or the neighbour about it in advance, do you? You wait till afterwards. It's just the same with rolling up a bit on the late side.

Now suppose Tom has totally and utterly forgotten that he has been bidden to dinner and the phone rings at 8.45pm just as he and his wife are finishing a delicious supper of scrambled eggs and crispy bacon. He answers the call. What should he say? A few suggestions:

1. I told your secretary this afternoon. We are just leaving for the airport now to collect the coffin.
2. We are so worried about our tortoise that our date for this evening slipped my mind.

3. Of course I haven't forgotten, but you've got the date wrong. We are coming to you tomorrow and much look forward to it.
4. I have spent half the afternoon trying to ring you but kept getting misrouted to Clarence House. What a charming old lady the Queen Mother is, to be sure. Long may she be with us. Anyway, sorry to let you down. Must fly. Pip pip.
5. You haven't heard? Oh, I thought you were ringing up to commiserate. Everything was in it. Credit cards, cheque book, cigarettes and, of course, my diary. Oh, I think it's a bit late now, don't you?

The Ashes to Ashes Guest

The Irish Guest from the lower regions, to whit Nick O'Tine, asks if he can smoke. If the host says no, he then points out to his host that just as he as a good guest must always be polite and ask, the good host must always be polite and say "Yes".

If he is aware in advance that not even such a profound observation as this will weaken his host's resolve to preserve his house as a smoke-free zone then he does not ask, but contents himself with lighting up and saying in due course, "For the sake of your carpets do you think I could have something in which to stub out my cigarette? An ashtray perhaps?"

The smoking guest should bear in mind that nowadays not all women understand that when you blow smoke in their faces this is a form of foreplay. Women, particularly Americans, tend to consider that this charming and intimate gesture constitutes an attempt to kill them.

Life has become very hard indeed for the smoking guest. The practice of having a quick drag between each course is not now much favoured – particularly at white-tie City dinners. The guest who fancies lighting up between the brown Windsor and the grey

This charming and intimate gesture is considered by Americans to constitute an attempt to kill them...

mullet may have to plead a prostate condition and whip smartly off to the gents.

Nick always offers his cigarettes around to the assembled company. This generous gesture is most unlikely to deprive him of a cigarette but could well cause any Americans present to have an apoplectic fit. Apoplectic fits can be terminal.

So perish all prunes. Of course cigarettes can be terminal too. Life is crazy, is it not?

⟶ *The Hippocratic Guest* ⟵

Dr Laidlow, the medical guest, is only too well aware of the tribulations which his profession may suffer at dinner parties. Hardly has he removed his anorak but a fellow guest, not previously known to him, sidles up. "Hear you're a GP." He removes his shoes and socks. "Forgive me, I am a busy man." (This infers quite clearly that our doctor friend devotes his day to painting his toe-nails and reading *Vogue*.) "Do put my mind at rest. Are these ..." he asks, as he walks all over the carpet in bare feet, "contagious? I mean are they what you chaps call verrucas?" He obviously has his own pet name for them.

Dr Laidlow returns to his car to retrieve his bag. By means of a magnifying glass in his rubber-gloved hand he studies the craters on the underside of his fellow guest's size elevens. He draws his breath in sharply. "And how long has this pretty little kettle of fish been going on? Three or four months, eh? What a tragic twist of fate. This little get-together might so easily have taken place even a few weeks ago. I think there would then have been a reasonable chance of catching things in time." "In time?" Our footsore friend is somewhat under-joyed.

"Let me explain. There are," he is now getting nicely into his stride, "various forms of verruca, the most prevalent of which is the verruca communus muddus or verruca simplex. This fellow, although inclined to spread, is comparatively simple to treat. We then have the verruca non-tropo male which can be a little hairy, but usually responds to surgery under general anaesthetic, sometimes involving removing the sole of the foot. Lastly, and alas not least, we have the verruca horribilis. This is very rare. In fact," he again studies the guest's foot with his glass, "I am not sure I have ever seen one before, let alone seven." The party is now listening with bated breath while the guest himself is giving a splendid impression of a stunned mullet.

"And the prognosis?" his lips are trembling, his face is ashen. His hand shakes so much that most of the contents of his tumbler do not reach his lips. "Later," Dr Laidlow announces, in tones that brook no argument, "Let the rest of us enjoy the fair Cynthia's culinary arts first. But this I will say. Put that glass down. You must never even smell alcohol again." The poor man, a lush in oenophile's clothing, is, at the thought that his gob will never again be smacked by the cup that inebriates but does not cheer, all but totally destroyed.

At the table, the hired help makes towards him with the Meersault. The doctor waves her imperiously on. By the time the Petrus arrives the guest is using his double damask to wipe away a tear.

"Not even the tiniest taste?"

"You will be taking your life in your hands; and by the way no goose liver, fish roe or shellfish – particularly lobsters or oysters from now on. Plenty of muesli."

"Hate it."

"And haggis."

"Can't bear the stuff."

"And green peppers."

"Can't swallow them."

"Basically as much yoghurt as you can possibly get down. No golf or chocolates. I will discuss the question of sexual intercourse in detail with you when we can have a private moment. I shall, *inter alia*, be telling you that, for the sake of your partner, when making love you should both wear wellingtons throughout."

By now the stricken guest's wife has slid her shoes under the table and is nervously feeling under her feet.

"Do you all like coffee?" perks up Cynthia who has found the evening most entertaining. She has never had too much time for the afflicted guest, he being invariably garrulous by the soup, argumentative over the sorbet, totally insufferable by the cheese and rotten to his wife over the brandy. Mind you, he is a different man tonight. The doctor intervenes, "I am sure the rest of us would love coffee. My friend here would like decaffeinated herbal tea."

As the two of them walk back together to the drawing room he asks the doctor if there is any treatment.

"Nothing orthodox, I am afraid. At medical school we were taught that in most cases verruca horribilis simply runs its course."

"Runs its course?" the guest is at his tether's end.

"Spreads."

"Everywhere? Hands?"

"Very much so. Then of course you will have to wear rubber gloves as well as the wellingtons. There is acupuncture. Normally acupuncture is painless but they have to go into the very heart of the verruca. Do you have a high pain threshold? By jove look at the hour. I must wend my way. Anyway in your condition you should not be too late in bed."

The party breaks up. The doctor stands in the doorway making polite noises to his host and hostess and bidding a cheery farewell to one and all.

"My last word to you, dear boy, is to tell you a brief story. I think it was F.E. Smith or it could have been Lord Birkenhead. Someone asked him for a legal opinion over the crêpes Suzettes. So he told him a great heap of "how's-your-father" and just as he was going he said, 'Sir, my opinion is worth exactly what it has cost you; if you want proper advice come and see me in my chambers.' How I wish this were true in your case and that you had perfectly ordinary common or garden verrucas. But," he paused, "to be absolutely certain why not come and see me during surgery hours tomorrow and I'll have another look?"

He did. Since that day he has never tried to get free advice from anyone at a dinner party.

⟿ *The Guest from Hell and Intensive Care* ⟿

Mark Malinger does not like to waste the substantial annual investment he makes in BUPA.

He has, in his time, attempted to stay in various fatty farms at their expense, pointing out that as the state sector is in the habit of sending teenage criminals on luxury cruises, the least private enterprise can do is to allow him to become less disease-prone by spending a few relaxing days at Forest Mere.

As he has not been all that successful in these laudable attempts to persuade the British United Provident Association to be true to its name and allow him to indulge in this particular form of preventive medicine, he is forced to take other measures.

So it is that two or three times a year he convinces his gullible quack that he is in need of a few tests, possibly culminating in minor surgery, and he adjourns with his fax, video, Windows '95, talking books and CDs to the Wellington. Anywhere else would be unthinkable. "My dear," he said on one occasion to his medical adviser, "have you never taken the trouble to read the wine list at the Royal Free? Even a passing glance could turn a carefree soul into a manic-depressive." Preferably any surgery is of a keyhole nature. Not being a Stuttgart university alumunus he does not consider that hideous scars would add to his manly charm.

Ideally, he goes in for observation, i.e. to observe the nurses and arrange for one or two of them to do a little moonlighting. He tries to slot his visit in just after his return from the Seychelles. A good all-over tan is essential if he is to look his most attractive when attired only in an identification tag around his wrist. Comforted by the fact that BUPA will be defraying the amazing cost of his accommodation he does not stint himself. A certain advance outlay is required if the operation, in the general sense of the word, is to be a success.

He does not, for instance, rely on well-wishers coming up trumps. No indeed. He comes up trumps for himself. By the time he arrives in his private room it is awash with orchids, pot plants and corsages of all sorts from Ken Turner, and other such irreproachable florists.

"Ah," he remarks to matron, who has reacted very positively to Mark's temporary abode being turned into an annexe to the Chelsea Flower Show, "Princess Michael never misses a trick, does she? So wonderfully preserved and deliciously Teutonic.

"Ah, what have we here? A case of Mouton from Jacob. So kind. And who sent these ravishing blooms? Luciano. I should have guessed. I do wish the dear man would not fiddle so incessantly with his hankie, don't you, matron?" She is, of course, crashing snob that she is, entranced. Such a relief after all those Arabs with armed guards patrolling the corridors. He settles down, safe in the knowledge that his every whim will be catered for – a midnight massage perhaps from the red-headed Irish staff nurse, with the Do Not Disturb notice hanging from the door-handle. On matron's orders said red-head does her very best to help him unwind.

Buck's Fizz and salmon fishcakes at 9am. Why not? Such a lovely man. A tall blonde out-of-work actress is shown in, in a yashmak. Mark bows from the neck. As she leaves matron tells her how much her flowers were appreciated. Matron realises that Her Royal Highness must sometimes travel incognito and Mark's rating reaches an all-time high.

Eventually, it is time for him to take his leave. He returns the case of Mouton to Berry Bros. He carries under his arm the weighty volume of X-rays which show him to be the very epitome of good health and which ensure that were he ever to want life insurance, which in fact he never would, it would be offered to him at a knock-down rate. So that he may remain in tip-top condition and not expose himself to the infectious diseases and expense that are involved in transport by taxi, the hospital is dropping him off at Heathrow in an ambulance so that he may return to the Seychelles to complete his convalescence. As he leaves, the staff of his wing, his surgeon, anaesthetist and matron, the red-headed nurse with the mole just above her pubic hair, team line his corridor and applaud respectfully. He finds this pausette in the rush of day-to-day guesting much better value that the annual check-up offered by BUPA. £252 for a stool test. Outrageous.

The Not-firing-on-all-cylinders Guest

Phillip Pheeling-Yuckie (known to his intimates as Ill Phil) never lets down those who have favoured him with an invitation.

Be he yet burdened with a hacking cough and invited to Covent Garden, he is right in there. Duty calls. Be he laid low with influenza and summoned for the weekend to an elderly party hanging on to life by a thread, he does not even consider letting her down; in fact he favours her with the sort of kiss that evokes in her both fond memories and grim forebodings.

Should a better invitation arrive subsequently then his indisposition does provide an impeccable excuse for declining the earlier one. Otherwise no minor ailment such as conjunctivitis (very catching), a chronic nose bleed (I may have to nip out after the main course for a quick transfusion. In the meantime might my fillet be *saignant*?), or a really chesty cold (might I keep your Qian

"Good gracious! I do believe I'm getting one of my stinkers — not that I ever let a fever interfere with my social life..."

Long cuspidor at hand for the evening?) will dissuade him from rolling up. A free meal is, after all, a free meal.

His technique is to appear sneezing profusely over one and all and announce, "Good gracious, I do believe I am getting one of my stinkers." Shortly afterwards, while bravely quaffing a pre-prandial Scotch of medicinal proportions ("a little hot lemon and barley if you have it"), he will produce a thermometer from his top pocket and, placing it in his mouth, proceed to hum the Dead March from *Saul*. "104. Good gracious. Never mind. We Pheeling-Yuckies never let a fever get us down."

Then there is the mystery complaint. This can really make the party go with a swing while they all discuss it. He starts off low-key. "Could I trouble you for a glass of water? It's just for a pill. I don't know why I bother. They seem to have absolutely no effect. What are they? A cocktail of antibiotics. What the medics give you when they are stumped. Evidently it may or may not be catching. Some sort of virus I dare say. Remember Charlie Croaker? I saw him the week before last, just after he got back from Lagos. Only with him a few minutes. His funeral was last Thursday. His GP had no idea what to put on his death certificate – forgive me – was that your glass? They have, you will be happy to hear, more or less ruled out meningitis. When I say more or less ... forgive the pullover, I do get a bit shivery."

By now every hypochondriac in the room is shivering in sympathy.

Then there is the question of not being well enough to leave, as in *The Man Who Came to Dinner* which was about a man who broke his leg. Our Phillip does not break a leg. He develops mumps. Total darkness. Highly infectious. Special diet. As he recovers he finds himself just able to stagger down to the sitting room to watch *Red Hot Dutch* on satellite television. He, of course, speaks Dutch. His host and hostess do not. Never mind, they can always do the *Times* crossword, if only they did not have to sit in total darkness because of his mumps. And if only he had not already done it for them to save them the trouble.

Meanwhile he has to do his best, poor fellow, to keep his business going. Luckily they have a fax. During business hours he needs sole use of it. He also needs sole use of the telephone at all times. Hardly has the Stock Exchange closed in New York but things open up in Tokyo and Sydney. The phone rings throughout the night. The office is in constant touch and his lissom secretary pops up to his darkened bedroom with various papers. Apparently she has had mumps.

Eventually it is time to make an exit so that he may convalesce with friends in Nevis. Anyway his hostess has now developed mumps.

On occasions Phillip arrives at a party in rude health. This does not necessarily mean that he proceeds to be rude to everyone. It may of course. He does not believe in shrinking from giving the kiss of life to an evening threatened with rigor mortis. When it comes to conversation he prides himself on possessing the talents of a picador. A *double entendre* here, an innuendo there and in no time he has sought out areas of bitter disagreement amongst his fellow guests. The ultimate goal, of course, is to bring into the open that philosophical chasm between host and hostess that has been simmering away these last thirty years. So that he could be provided with his creature comforts and she could shop till well after she dropped they have managed to hang together by a thread. They do, of course, have certain things in common. No couple can disagree about everything. *Par example* they are both attracted to younger men. But basically there are huge areas of conflict simply screaming for an airing. It only takes a few idle queries and the atmosphere becomes supercharged. The tension quickly encompasses the entire party, which really starts to go with a swing. Soon lifelong friendships are reaching their conclusion. High Court judges are wondering what some of the names they are being called mean. Husbands are leaving their wives. Bankers are leaving the country. With luck, by the end of the evening, there will not be a throat at which someone has not been.

Simply because Phillip arrives in rude health there is no reason why he should stay that way. He may be sitting over coffee, having at last joined the ladies, when he overhears his hostess unwillingly sharing with a guest the recipe for the excellent fish pie they have consumed an hour or two earlier. "I trust, dear lady, my ears were deceiving me. Aware as you surely are of my allergy, you are not saying there were prawns hiding coyly in that otherwise impeccable dish?"

Within minutes of failing to be reassured he has thrown up over the Aubusson, fainted, knocking over and smashing as he does so a priceless Etruscan vase, and is on his way to the London Clinic. After a week or so, when he feels sufficiently rested, he will return home and in due course post off the preposterous bill to his hosts.

As his last words when the ambulance arrived at the party had been "culpable homicide" they regard £7,000 as a small price to pay for the safe return to health of their dear friend, who was in fact suffering from gastroenteritis. Tests carried out at the Clinic establish once and for all that nothing agrees with him better than shellfish. Being a considerate fellow he writes the moment he has banked her cheque to tell his hostess this, so that she can, if she so wishes, give him her set piece fish pie on a future occasion without changing the recipe. It is these thoughtful touches that have made him so sought after as a guest.

"Himself" and Cocktail Parties

Cocktail parties are a sort of punishment which you inflict upon your less close friends. What makes matters worse is that you usually hold a cocktail party to "work off" those to whom you owe hospitality. You rarely just owe them for a cocktail party. Often they have had you to dinner and you can't quite think of anyone they would go with, so for them and their like you throw this huge thrash in a confined space (praying most of them won't turn up) and give them hundreds and hundreds of stuffed Californian prunes washed down by a rather nasty fizzy wine, its identity a secret closely guarded by a white napkin.

"Himself" never throws cocktail parties. He never throws any parties actually. He is quintessentially and forever a guest.

He follows certain rules where cocktail parties are concerned and these rules depend on the answer to certain questions.

1. Who is giving the party?
2. Does he already know the host's friends?
3. If not, does he wish to meet them?
4. If so, does he like them?
5. Are the likely guests going to be names worth dropping or just

worth dropping, period? Can he dine out on them? As he spends his life dining out, this is important.

6. Do the hosts
   a. make the eats themselves?
   b. get a friend's daughter to knock them up a week in advance in between breast-feeding the latest arrival?
   c. buy them at Marks and Spencer's?
   d. use Mustard Catering or Tina Blick? . . .

   (c. would be just about bearable; d. would be a joy).

7. So far as drink is concerned is it by any chance a Pimms party? A total no-no; always made too weak.

If the invitation merely announces that the hostess is at home and will be providing "drinks" 6–8pm, then not much more can be done. Although "himself" does not know the meaning of fear he simply cannot ring up his hostess in advance and say, "When you say drinks would you be a little more specific. If you mean vintage Moët count me in, Heidsieck and it's a definite maybe, Lonsdale Ridge Australian Chardonnay and alas there is no way I can make it."

THE COCKTAIL PARTY TECHNIQUE

The uninitiated guest is all too familiar with the horror of the average cocktail party. He (or indeed she) arrives at the entrance. He sees no one he knows except his host, who appears to be clinching some vast deal with Richard Branson. Not the moment to interrupt. He spots a pretty self-assured face. He knows her. The only trouble is that she does not know him. No joy there. His hostess descends on him. "Lovely to see you, you must come and meet . . . " And so he is put in to bat with the most boring member of the party. As no one else will talk to her he is with her for keeps. He listens as she refers to an endless list of celebrities by their Christian names. Frantically he looks over her shoulder. His

"When you say 'DRINKS' – if you mean vintage Moët, count me in, Heidseick, and it's a definite maybe and Lonsdale Ridge Australian Chardonnay and, alas, there is no way I can make it..."

eyes plead for help. He has a brainwave – "Must shed a tear for Lady Hamilton." He locks himself in the loo for ninety seconds and skims a well-thumbed copy of *Architectural Digest*. He pulls the plug and re-emerges.

"Now where were we?" she trills. "I was just telling you about my weekend with Jeffrey and Mary. I adore his books, don't you?" Pray God may the hostess appear out of the blue and swizzle him. But while the big guns are dragged around to meet and impress the little guns, the tiny guns – the toy guns – are left to fend for themselves. And so after a glass or two and a nibble or two he makes his excuses, interrupts his hostess only briefly to thank her for a wonderful cocktail party and makes his way home via a Chinese takeaway.

He might, of course, not have come alone. He might have brought a wife, in which case they can compare notes. "Did you meet Simon Jenkins?" "No." "Nor did I but we must remember to tell the children he was there." "Did you meet anyone amusing?" "Well, I had a brief word with Alastair Morton but when I told him I was one of his shareholders he sort of vanished." "Ah."

Now we come to "himself". Needless to say he makes mincement of cocktail parties. The moment the invitation arrives he sets about telephoning or accidentally bumping into those others he reckons have qualified for an invitation. There is nothing he enjoys more than putting his foot in it. "I thought you were pretty thick with the Woodham-Brownes. I am staggered they have not asked you. What could you have done? How sad. They give such smashing parties."

Eventually, having tracked down the chairman of a large public company, whose shareholders have foregone most of their dividend to allow him to live the life of Riley – and in particular to have a car and driver permanently on hand – "himself" implies that he will be in their neck of the woods that evening and could he cadge a lift?

Thus he arrives in a limo with the VIP and is snapped instantly for *Hello!* magazine. As he alights he has a few words with the driver, thereby giving the impression the car is his. The VIP is not photographed for *Hello!* magazine.

Once inside he removes a glass of champagne from the tray, sniffs it, replaces it and asks for whisky, "on the rocks, like the businesses of most people here under this Government," well knowing that the Chancellor of the Exchequer is at his elbow.

In no time at all he is engaging him in conversation and pulverising him with a series of statistics and initials. One thing about "himself" is that he does take the trouble to do his homework. The moment he knew the Chancellor was due to attend he had the city editor of *The Economist* to dinner at his club.

In due course the two of them are joined by some of the other leading lights, whose brief is to prise the poor Chancellor free. Easier said than done. Even when he has bludgeoned a weekend at Dorneywood out of the poor fellow, the Chancellor is not set free. "What," says the Foreign Secretary to the Chancellor, "are you doing afterwards?" "Himself" is about to inflict himself upon them for dinner, but he resists the temptation. He might well be asked to pay his share.

SUGGESTED TOPICS OF CONVERSATION FOR
COCKTAIL PARTIES

1. One's host's taste in furniture.
2. One's host's taste in children.
3. One's host's taste in guests.
4. One's host's taste in stuffed prunes – animate and inanimate.
5. One's host's taste in waitresses.
6. Is there life after death?
7. Is there life after cocktail parties?
8. Is there life after marriage?
9. Are you married?
10. Are you happily married? If not, when can we lunch?

Prunes - animate and inanimate...

1. Don't bother to come out of the closet, I'll join you there.
2. I can't think why our lovely hostess prefers lump fish roe to caviar.
3. Waitress dear, I am just popping up to the main bedroom for a rest. Would you be so kind as to let me have the odd nibble from time to time?

⟶ *The Guest from Hell* ⟵
and Wedding Invitations

Our hero, on retrieving his *Times* from the door mat and returning to bed with it, wastes little time on the births. He does attend the occasional christening but takes the greatest possible care never to become a godfather. Expensive business being a godfather. Rather, having regained his bed and switched on his Teasmade he repairs, prior even to the crossword, to a careful study of the engagements.

Many of those who choose to inform readers of their offspring's success in hooking some spotty young creature who will stare forever (or until death do them part) at a green screen in order to satisfy the inordinate demands of their plain, dim daughter can be ignored. Their names provide an important clue. If the father's first name is Ernest, forget it. If their surname is anything like Cluff or Branson, look no further.

Every now and then, he spots a name that rings a bell. He rushes to his carefully preserved copy of *The Sunday Times Top 500*. He reaches for *Who's Who*. He leafs through *Debrett's*. A property magnate perhaps. A merchant banker. A pop star. Or it could be a titled personage. Careful there. He would not wish to waste his valuable time upon some impecunious earl, unless, of course, he had succeeded in using his one remaining asset to ensnare some only child of a scrap metal merchant. That could be interesting. "The engagement is announced between Piers, eldest (good, the heir) son of Major-General and Lady Auden of Standeasy House, Pirbright, and Tracey, only daughter of Charles (Tippy) Boondyke of Megabuck Hall, Chalfont on Stour."

Instantly he places pen on parchment. *Who's Who* provides Lady Auden's first name. "Dear Tilly," he writes, "you must be delighted. I do not of course know Tippy Boondyke personally, although his name does pop up from time to time in the *FT*. I have such fond memories of Piers. Pass on messages to him. In fact tell him 'well done'. Well and truly off your hands if you know what I mean. Bung-ho. I will do my utmost to be in England for the wedding. Yours ever, Dieter A. Paartade, Jo'burg."

The poor demented Matilda Auden will of course be inundated with such letters. Wearily she will tell the temp she has hired to help her cope, "I can't remember him from a bar of soap. Add him to the list and we'll pray he can't get away from South Africa. I know Tippy can afford it but matters are getting out of control."

In due course the invitation arrives to join the serried ranks already festooning his mantelpiece. They make a splendid display and would be even more numerous, were not the crinkly edged ones kept discreetly out of sight.

— *And So to Wed* —

When your average, run-of-the-mill, not-too-much-loot-to-spare-but-must-do-the-decent-thing-within-reason guest opens the dreaded envelope and one of those no-expense-spared embossed numbers drops out, he heaves a sigh. Bye-bye to a Saturday. Can he still get into late Uncle Ernest's morning dress? What is the least he can get away with present-wise? "They were," he observes to his wife, "shacked up together quite happily. What on earth persuaded them to do this dreadful thing?" She suggests that it might be something to do with income tax. He then goes through the motions, emerging poorer (the wedding turns out to be at a pretty little church just outside Scunthorpe – the nearby hotel doing a special deal for guests, i.e. adding 20 per cent to its normal charges) and little wiser. They knew weddings were hell before they went.

Not so our hero.

Nowadays lots of weddings take place at 4pm or so, nibbles, cake and speeches all being disposed of by 7.30pm. This is the cue for wrinklies, geriatrics, dusties (i.e. anyone over forty) and those without seven-figure incomes to depart, leaving the young and the chosen few to sit down to a slap-up dinner and dance the night away. The thought that our hero has long since taken on board is that it is almost impossible to tell someone to go. Hints will be dropped. Our hero is a past (and present) master when it comes to ignoring hints. He has a skin off which a rhinoceros-piercing bullet would bounce effortlessly.

"No, as a matter of fact I haven't got a pressing engagement this evening ... you say a lot of people seem to be taking their leave. I expect they have pressing engagements. Have I enjoyed the wedding? Yes indeed, so far so good as you might say ... Why don't I piss off? Frankly there was such a queue at the Portaloo that I decided to cross my legs for a bit."

He will, of course, carry a place card with his name on in his top pocket; but let us to the wedding itself ...

He arrives at the church/chapel/temple/synagogue/aero-plane hangar or whatever in excellent time – preferably before the ushers. Due to the extraordinary variety of exploding eider-downs and Mad-Hatter stovepipes worn by young fashion victims, he, not being of inordinate height, will be quite unable to leer at the bride or groom (depending upon his persuasion) unless he is rubbing shoulders with the family. He will, of course, when the parents of the groom duly arrive, adopt his South African accent and introduce himself as cousin Dieter from Jo'burg.

Sometimes he rings the changes. Arming himself with a video camera he joins the bridal procession, giving a wave and a wink, as he moves up the aisle, to anyone worth waving or winking at.

Once the service is under way he chooses some vantage point which will let him shoot the event from an interesting angle; the altar perhaps, or the organ. This will enable him to capture the more intimate parts of the ceremony, the groom's mother in floods of tears at the thought of her Piers marrying a commoner. That sort of thing.

He should participate freely in the service. When the officiating priest tells the congregation that if any person present knows of any reason why these two should not be joined together in holy matrimony he should speak now or forever hold his peace, he calls out, taking care to maintain his South African accent, "they are both in the clear so far as I am concerned" and when the priest says, "those whom God has joined together let no man put asunder" he should add, "nor any woman for that matter". This may well elicit an appreciative murmur from any member of the Equal Opportunities Commission who happens to be present. When the priest says, "you may kiss the bride" he does not hesitate to do so.

Breaking the ice with total strangers at a midday reception presents no serious problems. The art is not to mess around. Small-talk about the bride's mother's recent face-lift or the fact that the costs for the lavish reception have been covered by some particularly sophisticated insider trading are frankly boring. This is the tedious tittle-tattle in which almost every other surrounding clique will be indulging. No; the Guest from Hell makes his new acquaintances sit up and take notice. "I'd like," he infers, having introduced himself as cousin Dieter, "to be a fly on the wall or even better to be on the other side of a two-way mirror during their honeymoon. She'll teach dear old Piers a thing or two. Yes, indeed. She certainly completed my education between the covers. She came out and stayed with me in South Africa when she was fifteen. She was a goer, I can tell you. I used to call her Vesuvius. A Yankee pal of mine met her while he was in Jo'burg without his wife. He called her his English Muffin. They don't have crumpets in the States, you know. Well, I must move on and spread the word. Nice talking to you."

He considers large formal weddings to be hugely diverting. The sight of all that money being poured down the drain on a union which is not likely to persist beyond a few months is, he finds, one of life's great joys. And the excruciating plainness of some of the young females – and indeed males – who make it to the altar. One of the wonders of the world. Nothing to do with their parents' means of course.

Weddings can also be extremely useful. By the time of the reception many of the better-looking females, used and unused, have mentally homed in on what weddings are all about. That is to say, relationships. The happy fiction of the young bride yielding up her virginity on the wedding night followed by two weeks of frenetic sexual activity between the sheets in the Seychelles. Never mind that the happy couple have been shacked up for two years, that he already has his own Camilla Parker Bowles (also a divorcee, who wanted to be a maid of dishonour at the wedding, but had to be restrained) and that the honeymoon will in fact be devoted to as much golfing in Scotland as may be safely under- taken, bearing in mind that she is six months pregnant.

Our hero was very touched to receive shortly before a recent wedding, scheduled for September, a charming card covered in tinsel and babies blowing bubbles and bearing a printed note, "Piers and Tracey are proud to announce that they are expecting a baby in January." Nothing like laying it on the line.

Never mind. It is the thought that stimulates the adrenalin. Those who are still on the market should be putty in his artistic hands.

As for the already wed:

Widows might, spinsters will
Married women easier still.

Of course, sex is not everything. No, no, no. There are other things in life that help one get one's breath back. For instance, weddings are perfect for meeting new people, charming them into the ground and fixing up all sorts of visits to Ascot, the South of France, Courcheval or just a simple dinner at Le Gavroche or Taillevent. Eurostar make the latter so easy. After all, he must be an OK sort of chap or he would not be at the wedding at all, would he?

The Guest Attends a Christening

"I christen this little child Clint"
Said the vicar, with hardly a hint
of disapprobation or grief –
But rather a sigh of relief
That the child should be christened at all.
The priest would have much preferred Paul
But no; he must suffer his stint
On this earth with the dread name of "Clint"
Poor Clint; but remember the Boss
'Tis an honour to carry a cross.

The Nuptual Gift
(RSVP = Remember Send Vedding Present)

A ticklish matter. The abominable guest takes a pride in spending the absolute minimum required to maintain the end in a vertical position.

Certain enquiries can be made. For instance, are the proud parents following that outdated and unspeakable custom of flaunting the glitzy trinkets at the reception? Posing as a reporter from *Hello!*, he enquires. They are? Excellent. The problem is solved. He takes a card emblazoned with Dieter's name, crest, South African address and best wishes, extracts it at the appropriate moment from the inside pocket of his morning dress, removes the donor's card from one of the classier objects – Paul Storr candlesticks perhaps – and substitutes his own.

The next best solution is to send nothing. Who will ever discover? As he never knew them in the first place he is most unlikely to bump into Piers or Tracey. Even if Tracey's parents do insist he joins them in their box to hear Pavarotti at the Garden and the kids roll up too, he will indulge in a little harmless fun during the interval. "Piers, old chap," he will murmur (as Piers racks his brain to remember where they met), "I take it, as my modest gift remains unacknowledged that it was never received. A trifle odd as I sent it recorded delivery. What was it? Just the teeniest weeniest bit of Fabergé. Perhaps it accidently fell into the wastepaper basket. Never mind. I expect you are knee-deep in Fabergé already. If it should turn up do let me know. It was an Easter egg encrusted in diamonds and rubies. It was left to me by an old boy whose life I saved. It never quite took root in my unpretentious pad. I was always worried in case it did a Humpty-Dumpty."

Of course, he may be about to attend the wedding of someone he actually knows – someone who is about to await the product of his munificence with bated breath. Will he repair to the GTC or whoever has custody of that dreadful document "The List"? No, he will not. They would then know what his gift had cost and that would never do.

He will start by foraging around the house, particularly in the attic and basement. Some appalling pottery plate presented to him by a long-departed Filipino au pair perhaps; a duplicate part set of the works of Kipling which his local bookseller has recently told him is of no commercial value. There is usually some object in a house the removal from which would improve it.

Then again, newlyweds can never have too much Tupperware. Dieter might well work off a few friends who have lent him their yachts or whatever by inviting them to a Tupperware party. He will then receive a quantity of these splendid containers as his commission which he will persuade Asprey to gift wrap and deliver to the happy couple.

— *Not Overdoing It* —

Percy Penny-Pinching would never dream of bearding a threshold empty-handed. Nor would he ever allow his mit to be overfull. He is probably the most sensitive soul ever to walk the planet. Or at least one of them.

Suppose he was embarking on a prolonged visit to the Lutine-Bells, a charming couple hit with a positively Tyson-like ferocity by Lloyd's. Other less thoughtful creatures might think it charitable in these circs to roll up bearing at the very least a cooked ham, a case of Haut-Brion '78, a wheelbarrow filled with garden produce including a pannier of truffles, a box of cartridges for him, a gold necklace for her and/or various other acceptable trifles.

But just suppose that on the very first evening of his sojourn, while the Lutine-Bells were still coming to terms with those reminders of the happy days when they too could afford such luxuries, the soufflé were to fail to rise, or the cat were to indulge in a pre-emptive strike on the smoked mackerel. Oh, the ashen faces. Ah, the abject apologies.

"When we think of what you have done for us."

"How," bleats the elderly Colonel Lutine-Bell, lately known to his entire regiment, except to his face, as "Squinty", "can I ever look you in the eye again?"

This of course would never do. To them that hath shall be given and from them that hath not... well, a small packet of smoked mackerel would about fit the bill. Most important to make friends with the cat. When the inevitable occurs, the phrase "easy come, easy go" springs to mind.

The truly successful gift should walk the razor's edge between the derisory and the vulgar.

Our guest's well-meaning generosity might so easily, if over-done, be taken as a tasteless way of outgunning, upstaging and generally sending off to slow music such well-meaning fellow guests as the Sevilles, who have, over the last three decades, never deviated from their practice of arriving with a modest-sized pot – it used to be the 1lb size for less than a week and the 2lb for longer – the only concession to changing times being that it is now 400 gms and 800 gms respectively. This pot contains a somewhat runny sub-stance and, being absolutely free from preservatives, has mould on top. It is inscribed, with devastating wit, "Old Mother Seville's Home Made Marmalade". The vintage is noted bottom right.

It would never do to make the Sevilles feel inadequate. Not that the Sevilles have fallen on hard times. They have never, due to Mr Seville's conviction that there was a fortune to be made out of his wife's home made marmalade, known anything else.

The Sevilles are, in fact, right in principle if in need of practice. The most valued gift, as Percy is hugely aware, should be the product, not of wealth, but of time, trouble and thought. Thus, with the aid of a box of coloured ribbons and some sealing wax it takes him but a trice to turn a matchbox into a Pierrot. The modest gift need only prove an embarrassment to the donee until the sandpaper on the side wears out. So many presents outstay their welcome.

Percy deprecates the growing practice – unless he himself is entertaining – which, like conversation to the deaf, is almost unheard of, of taking a little something when all you have been asked out to is dinner.

Flowers the next day are out of the question. Interflora has

"If that's the champagne that 'you know who' brought - be careful not to let any of it drip onto my furniture..."

circulated the state of Percy's bank account to all their members long ago. What then, does he, our master of every situation, bear in his well-bred hand on such tricky occasions?

Answer, a small, beautifully wrapped packet. Not for him, unless he has stumbled on a case in his cellar that is undoubtedly corked, the ritual bottle of New Zealand Chardonnay. "How lovely, our favourite." Or, more unthinkable still, a bottle of non-vintage champagne, of such inexpensiveness that not a drip should be allowed, even for an instant, to touch the furniture.

The beautifully wrapped package (Percy very carefully folds up and keeps the outer coverings of all the previous year's Christmas gifts) is of course left to be admired on the hall table until after his departure.

When his hosts then fall on it, tearing it apart with their bare hands, he just hopes they are suitably chuffed to find it contains a scratchcard. Better, you might say, but you probably wouldn't, to scratch hopefully than to arrive.

— *Presents of Mind* —

On the other hand, what sort of modest gift should our Percy bear with him when offering to spend a few days with some passing acquaintances who happen to be possessed of a conveniently placed residence, preferably with swimming pool and tennis court?

Any of the following would not come amiss:

1. Books signed by the author are always a runaway success. These can be picked up without too much difficulty in secondhand bookshops.
2. Even unsigned books, if chosen with imagination, can fill the bill most adequately. "I trust you have not already read *The History of the West Carmarthen Mountain Railways, Volume II*," intones Percy cheerfully. Trains interest everyone.

Taking a little something when all you've been invited to is dinner ~ The beautifully wrapped scratch card ~ ('better to scratch hopefully than to arrive'...)

3. Should a guest have ever found a publisher for his own meanderings he will doubtless have cluttering up the attic some few hundred remaindered copies which he snapped up at 75p each to save them being pulped. He should remove one from the pile, autograph it and point out to his host that it is a first edition.

4. If a guest is partial to glacé fruits, these make an excellent gift that will go down extremely well – mainly because he will eat most of them himself.

5. A little something from Ken Lane, transferred to an Asprey's box, will have the host's wife bringing the guest breakfast in bed and very possibly staying on for a few minutes.

6. A puppy. The guest will not be so foolish as to imagine that the fact that they do not own a dog means that they would not

want one. They have simply never got around to choosing one. He will on no account spoil the surprise by making any enquiries in advance. This lays the ground-work for many subsequent visits. For instance, an applica-tion form for a subscription to Pet Plan will be a welcome gift. No need to pay a fancy price for a pedigree animal, a cross between a Rottweiler and a Tibetan spaniel can be had for buttons.

7. What about the short, just passing through, visit of under ten days or so? How about swimming goggles? Particularly if they have their own pool. Swimming goggles have a certain versatility about them. They are extremely useful when driving those old MGs where you can put the windscreen down. And onion peeling becomes a piece of cake.

8. A rubber ball with a bell in it for the dog (see 6 above)..

9. A silver-plated box for the fifteen-year-old daughter of the house inscribed "A pill a day keeps the baby away".

10. A carton of Silk Cut for the host who has recently given up smoking on doctor's orders, "just in case you feel the need".

11. For the anorexic hostess, a slim tome entitled *How to lose 30lbs in a week.*

12. For the anti-blood sports daughter of an MFH, a year's supply of aniseed, a balaclava and a pick-handle.

13. What about the son and heir? Are Mum and Dad just a bit worried about him? Never out of his sister's glad rags? Bit too much after-shave? A good guide to Europe's most popular gay bars might go down a bundle.

14. Ashtrays. Some houses seem incredibly short of them – especially those belonging to asthmatics.

A FEW DONT'S PRESENT-WISE

1. A case of vintage champagne is a total no-no. This suggests the host cannot afford to buy his own or that the guest finds his

"... just a petit quelque-chose for my stunning and talented hostess — I trust you haven't already read 'The History of the West Camarthen Mountain Railways, Vol II ?...'"

host's champagne undrinkable. Such a gift implies that the host is ill bred, if not insolvent.

2. A tree or bush. This is particularly unsuitable if the host has no garden.

3. Scent. The implication is obvious. That the hostess is not nice to be near. This gift is almost as tasteless as the gift of deodorant for her husband.

4. Any food except glacé fruits. The Guest from Hell would thereby be implying that the last time he was kind enough to stop by, despite endless forays to the village in search of cream cakes and meringues he still lost half a stone.

5. Pairs of prints. Think of it. Every single time the donor writes to say he is on his way they will have to find out where the beastly things are, dig them out, dust them, take down their favourite Miró posters and fling them up instead.

"Dear Harold and Angela,

"Just a brief note from Cynthia and myself to thank you for a marvellous weekend. We enjoyed every minute of it. Had we remembered to put in our diaries that we were not expected until Saturday, how pitifully short it would have been. When we rolled up on Friday in time for drinks you, Angela, must have been surprised to say the least. Particularly as Harold was still at work and the head groom was giving you a massage. There I was, immaculate in my Paul Mitchell pomade and Garrick tie and there you were in your Carmen curlers, no make-up, one contact lens and no clothes. You were both dressed in no time and took it all in good part. Is Harold always late back on Fridays?

"It was great seeing the new house. A challenge. I can quite see why you moved, of course. Upwards House was not exactly cramped, but it did not adequately reflect the new post-share-option you, did it? Whereas having a stud for all those expensive racehorses does make a statement. I do admire the way you have hung on to and even display some of your original collection of biscuit tins and indeed the way you remain loyal to some, nay several, of the less important friends you made while you were still climbing the ladder.

"Do you remember the days when an entry in *Who's Who*, let alone *Debrett's*, seemed but a distant prospect? Life moves on. Many congratulations on your new job. I am sure you will make a success of it and end up in the Lords, if that is what you want. If that is what you really, really want, are you sure you are wise to remain a member of the Conservative party? Up to you of course.

"I am so desperately sorry about the red wine on the new carpet. As one of the other guests said, it will at least make the house look lived in. Wasn't that a hoot Camilla asking for white wine instead of champagne and the butler producing the Batard-Montrachet that was meant to go with the scallops at dinner? Tee, hee.

"You are so lucky owning a restaurant and being able to bring down the chef to do the cooking. What happens to the poor souls who go there while he is with you? Perhaps he pre-cooks a few dishes and freezes them.

"Not too many teething troubles in our bedroom. I can quite see why bedside tables would spoil the look of the room. As for the little window where the sun comes peeping in at morn; doubtless in the fullness of time you will get round to putting up some sort of curtain.

"Meanwhile it was just lovely to be with you and meet all your new and important pals. Best of luck with the low profile. I don't suppose you would fancy kitchen supper and a chat about old times. It doesn't seem a day since the two of you were living in that enchanting little place on the river with the bedroom built into the sitting room.

"Tir-rah, as Cilla would say, and once again – a great weekend.

"Yours,

"Your favourite guest.

"PS. When I was using your telephone (only for making telephone calls!) the eye happened to fall on the draft of your results to be published next week. Well done. I am now one of your shareholders."

— *Christmas Plans* —

Christmas in the view of Noel Scrounger-Good-Yule is not to be taken lightly. "My goodness me," he remarked to one of his syco-phants the other day – one Ferdinand Fotheringham, who went to an exceedingly minor public school and is in awe of Noel, who has always given him to understand that so far as he remembered he had been to Eton. Whenever he went to his club Noel always sought out one of the Fotheringhams of this world. He needed an audience and – much more important – he needed someone to pay for his drinks. He had got the "you really must let me pay for the next one" technique down to a very fine art.

"My goodness me," he repeated, "Christmas is upon us again. Christmas in my view is not to be taken lightly. No indeed."

As one would expect, Noel is positively drenched with masses of Yule-tide invitations each year. Choosing the wrong one can cost one dear. He begins by sifting through them.

The non-starters are committed, having been acknowledged, to the cylindrical receptacle under his desk. By mid-November a short-list has been arrived at. His thoughts are then marshalled on paper thus:

DRUMSPITTLE HOUSE, OWNED BY THE McSHIVERS

Setting – a perfectly frightful Victorian shooting lodge with a total absence of central heating, set in unattractive trees planted in regimented rows at the behest of the Forestry Commission. In dire need of modernisation and decoration throughout. One of the coldest manses in Scotland, and that's saying something. One is quite liable to be snowed in indefinitely, even supposing one has managed to get there in the first place.

Plumbing – No hope of a hot bath unless one catches the boiler unawares at 4.30am.

" I'm afraid that if you're hoping for a hot bath in this house you'll have to catch the boiler unawares at about four o'clock in the morning... "

Food – Various national dishes such as haggis, porridge, McDonald's etc. In general, splendid ingredients (such as Scotch beef) ruined by overcooking. As the joint will have to be carried across a mock Jacobean courtyard from some faraway kitchen it will almost be as cold as the house.

Drink – Non-stop. Only way of keeping warm. Treble malts for breakfast. Drambuie mid-morning. Château Montrose for lunch. Alka-Seltzer for tea. No toasts to "King over the water" as family are strict Presbyterians.

Company – Should mostly be in strait-jackets rather than kilts. Members of pagan tribes known as clans who make a habit of ignoring Christmas (due to Scots being allergic to giving presents?). They make a huge fist of a quaint ritual they call Hogmanay which occurs around 31st December and at which they go absolutely spare and drink endless cups of "kindness yet", with a bit of luck sobering up by mid-January. Other puzzling customs, e.g. first foot in.

Games – Highland games do not consist of charades, hat games, pub quizzes etc., but of projecting lengths of Forestry Commission timber across a field. Only safe after-dinner pastime is synchronised whisky drinking.

Outings – At this time of year tribal gatherings are held on neutral territory. These are called Caledonian Balls and can be very frightening experiences, high-pitched war-cries being uttered during ritual dances. For some strange reason upper-class skinheads who are all called Jamie are allowed to carry offensive weapons in their socks. These unpleasant implements are all called Dirk. Dresses must touch the ground (girls only).

Music – Should you hear a noise on Christmas morning which sounds uncommonly like a tomcat being operated on without an anaesthetic, and should your host later say, "did ye no hear the skirl of the pipes?", you should reply, "Aye" or "Aye, I did that."

The pipes referred to are unrelated to the sewage system and not an indication that the cesspit has just been emptied.

Conclusion – Away in a manger is one thing. Away in Scotland is another.

THE ROSARY

Once was enough. Who would have sussed that the Popes were left-footers? With nine children ranged from ten to one. Unremitting attendance by whole party at masses. Genuflections galore. Church a day's march away. Walls covered in cardinals. Host given to *ex cathedra* announcements about a little rain not hurting anyone as entire party frog-marched across swamp in storm. Message from Rome shown and recorded. Queen's Christmas broadcast not available, she being head of Church of England pro tem. Long queues for bathroom due to over-population.

DARLING POINT, SYDNEY

Turkey and all the trimmings over a barbie on Bondi Beach where the surf is deep and crisp and even, dressed only in a bikini and loads of sun cream to keep skin cancer at bay. Mince pies at sunset. What could be more romantic? Huge swarthy life-safers making passionate love to one another in between prizing pretty girls away from sharks in search of their Christmas dinner. Uncorking the champagne, mainly to get hold of the cork and tie it on to one's ten-gallon hat.

To cap the whole glorious experience, twenty-three hours of air travel – so long, of course, as the plane is on time.

The greatest joy of Christmas Down Under is that it finishes eleven hours earlier. Good on them.

THE COTTAGE, LIMPWRIST-ON-THE-DYKE, WILTS. HOME OF CYRIL MINCING-BY-CAMPLY WHEN NOT IN MOROCCO

Only when it was too late to make other arrangements was Noel told that on Boxing Day they always held a fancy dress party and that cross-dressing was the order of the day. Cyril himself could not bear to wait that long and greeted his guests already attired as the fairy on top of the Christmas tree. He greeted Noel warmly, leaving most of his lipstick behind on Noel's right cheek.

It has to be said that Noel found the whole event somewhat frustrating. Every dishy bird turned out to be either half a uni-sex item or all of a chap. In general he tried to steer well clear of the mistletoe. He went as Barbara Cartland and won a pair of earrings.

THE CASTLE, WINDSOR

Noel sends a note: "Dear Maj, Terribly kind thought – hate to let you down – regards to one and all – compliments of the Season – have a great time on Boxing Day – kill a few for me – always willing to buy out. Be lucky. Do well."

Well, he thought about it, but really. All those split homes. And all that brown Windsor. Mind you, there are consolations. Princess Michael for one.

MILLIONAIRE'S ROW, HAMPSTEAD, GLORIOUS HOME OF SIR IZZY WELLOFFSKI

Setting – Wonderful, if you like that sort of thing. OTT. Comfort on wheels. A Rubens here, a Rembrandt there, a Poussin almost everywhere. Security like Fort Knox, but can you wonder?

Plumbing – Impeccable.

Staff – In profusion and how lovely.

Drinks – An oenophile's dream, e.g. pre-phylloxera plonk. Probably an unassuming little pre-prandial Le Montrachet, but at the very worst an unpretentious Mersault. Petrus with the pastrami. Bechevelle with the bagel. One can struggle by.

Company – Thoroughly sensible people who send cards saying "have a nice holiday", do not dislocate the festivities by dragging you out at midnight to squeeze into a church that is empty the rest of the year and will probably have holiday pudding after the turkey.

Of course, if Christmas falls on a Friday ... by and large the Scrounger-Good-Yules of this world will opt for a Jewish Christmas any day.

⬤ *The Guest from Hell's Christmas Ode* ⬤

Perhaps this Yuletide, Cynthia,
You kindly will avoid
Referring to the starving,
The sick, the unemployed.

Turn up the central heating,
Enjoy the caviar
And the gold and myrrh and frankincense,
That cometh from afar.

Remember, Cynthia, Christmastime
Occurs but once a year
And is, by long tradition,
A festive time of year.

This being so one subject

That is absolutely banned
Is the fact that hypothermia
Is rampant in the land.

From Christmas Eve to New Year's Day
I trust you will agree
To outlaw battered babies
And the NSPCC.

Let us rather concentrate
Upon the caviar
And the stranger in the manger
Born underneath a star.

Supposing Christ was born this year
How splendid it would be;
We could watch the whole thing happening
Live upon TV.

If it should clash with Christmas lunch
We'd simply cry "Hooray"
And record it on the video
For later in the day.

The Guest from Hell
and the Dear Departed

THE HON. YORICK DE'ATH ADORES FUNERALS

There is no need to send a present before attending a funeral.
Flowers on the other hand are acceptable. Pot plants are not a
good idea. Throughout the year, somewhere in the country,

proud owners are opening their gardens to the public. They, being so keen on their cabbage patch that they wish to flaunt it, are invariably vulnerable to flattery. As flattery costs nothing Yorick dishes it out effortlessly and in profusion. A sigh of admiration over the begonias, a gasp at the roses, fulsome praise for the orchids and in a trice he is being inundated with cuttings which make up nicely into a wreath.

The normal dress for a funeral is black tie, i.e. mourning dress. The invitation is unlikely to give any guidance for the simple reason that written invitations are not sent out in the case of funerals. Which is, like funerals, rather sad.

> *Mrs Gerald Snodgrass*
> *has great pleasure in inviting*
>
> ....
>
> *to the funeral of her late husband*
> *Colonel Gerald Snodgrass, CVO, Rtd, (now expd)*
> *at St Mary's, Hamilton Terrace*
> *on Wednesday April 1st at 5pm*
> *and afterwards at 49 Clifton Hill, NW8.*

Gun Carriages 1am.

Cremations are particularly poignant. Yorick, whose one great talent in life is a rudimentary ability to play the organ, always makes a point not just of offering his services but of actually insisting on taking over, however much this puts the nose of the incumbent tinkler of the consecrated ivories out of joint. He does this because he has up his sleeve a considerable repertoire of tunes designed to comfort those close to the frazzled in their hour of grief. "I don't want to set the world on fire, I just want to start a flame in your heart" is but one of them. The congregation then files out to the theme from *Chariots of Fire*.

Small-talk is not easy at a wake but needless to say Yorick is up to it. "A good innings," he will remark cheerfully to a fellow guest who happens to be the same age as the poor fellow who has just been incinerated.

"I wonder if 'Sticky' ever got round to telling you that he wanted me to have his Purdeys," he will murmur to the widow. "No rush. If the key to the gun-safe is not to hand I can always drop around tomorrow. I wish I could stay longer. Thanks for the most marvellous party. And do pass my thanks on to Sticky. He does not seem to be around at the moment. Silly me. I keep forgetting that he has, as it were, come to a sticky end."

THE GUEST FROM HELL
AND MEMORIAL SERVICES

Memorial services come very high on Yorick's list of priorities, particularly those that are admission by ticket only. The first thing he does on arrival at the church is to buttonhole the *Times* reporter and give him his name, diffidently informing him that he is the Hon. Yorick De'ath. This should put him above all the mere misters when the guest list is published in *The Times* the following day.

He arrives in extremely good time. Having placed a towel on the pew immediately behind that occupied by the family, he pins his laser-printed "usher" badge onto his lapel and proceeds to seat the various guests. He will restrain himself from asking whether the guests are bride or groom, concentrating instead on whether they were intimate with the deceased on account of their common interest in golf, bridge, S&M, the Tory party, cross-dressing, the NSPCC, paedophilia, hunting or massage parlours, and placing them accordingly.

Yorick, having allocated most of a morning of his valuable time to this exercise, would not want his presence to go unnoticed or unappreciated. This being so he will punctuate the interminable address with a series of speak-ups and hear-hears.

"did Sticky ever get round to telling you he wanted me to have his Purdeys? No rush – if you haven't got the key to the gun room on you now, I'll drop by tomorrow..."

It is not, by and large, the fault of widows that they tend to outlive their husbands.

It can be of course. One does *de temps en temps* meet spouses who appear to be intent on shortening their partners' spans in every way that the most fertile imagination could conceive. Whenever a male septuagenarian tells you he has just taken up hang-gliding or microlighting you can bet your sweet bippy that:

a. He has a heart condition.
b. She is at least ten years younger than him.
c. She has just started an affair with an Italian toy-boy.
d. She suggested it.

The dismissal of a husband who is clearly reaching the age where he is going to be more of a liability than an asset can be expedited by incessant reminders of his mortality.

"Where shall we go for our summer hol, always supposing …"

"Hello, is that the Golders Green crematorium? Could you pencil in Tuesday the 23rd?"

"I don't like the look of him. Dear, I didn't realise you were in the room."

"Don't touch those chocolate chip cookies. They're for the wake."

There is, of course, ground glass in the spinach, a tripwire at the top of the stairs, or for a more direct approach, the twelve-bore.

However blameless the relict may be for the demise of her beloved, the bachelor or widower guest is somewhat chary of seeking out her company. That she has been enormously plucky he does not doubt. One of the troubles tends to be that they did work awfully well as a team. He used to make the coffee.

At the appropriate moment the relict, who has been consoling herself by having an affair with Johnny Walker, i.e. has put away four strong ones, shouts, "Hands up if anyone wants coffee." Every guest dutifully raises a mit skywards. That tends to be it.

Relicts tend to economise; partly because their late husbands usually took total charge of all matters financial and partly because the saying "you can't take it with you" tends to be codswallop. His generous pension ensured that they lived in some style. He had not bothered to tell his wife that the annuity he had purchased with his shares was solely in his name. His neglect to keep up his BUPA subscription had cost them dear. His operations, the twenty-four-hour nursing, the months in hospital. She had floated the idea of going NHS. He had looked so deeply, deeply hurt.

The Guest from Hell does occasionally come across an exception. "I never realised Harold was so loaded. What a mean old stick he was. I cannot think why I kept him alive so long. I should have withdrawn his life-support machine years ago. Do have some more Latour and I have a spare seat in my box for Domingo next Tuesday." The trouble with most widows is that they no longer have a husband around to tell them when to shut up. When it is Latour and Domingo on the other hand their absence can be tolerated.

⟶ *Our Guest Bids Farewell to a Great Shot* ⟵

It was, in his opinion and that of his fellow guns, our hero remarked to his pal Frothy, thoughtless in the extreme of Stiffy Parkinson-Plute to have taken his premature departure from this life right in the middle of the shooting season, he being a mere child of ninety-two winters.

He had taken his leave of them, he continued, if not in style then at least with some degree of panache. After all, anyone can accidentally pop a twenty-bore cartridge into a twelve-bore. Nothing special about that. Being struck on the back of the neck by a vengeful pheasant falling from a great height also smacks somewhat of the commonplace.

What made Stiffy's exit a whit less run-of-the-mill was that he was waving something other than his Purdey at the not unattractive keeper's wife when rigor mortis set in rather suddenly. Just before that excellent Berry Bros. tipple Kings Ginger was due to make its mid-morning appearance. "Dear old Stiffy. True to the end – as you might say. Sad matter. It all happened immediately before the big drive of the morning.

"Stiffy would have been on number five – the hot seat. A couple of beaters thoughtfully carried him there and set him up on his shooting stick. As wave after wave of pheasants flew directly above him, everyone cried 'Over' but not unnaturally he did not respond. For him it *was* over. Some of the birds dipped their wings in salute. He had been a great shot in his day, had Stiffy.

"Stiffy's widow, a mature Swede of at least thirty-eight, named Ursula, insisted that the funeral should take place on a Saturday and not any old Saturday, but the very Saturday on which tradition decreed they did Home Park. Notwithstanding which, Ursula would not budge. That, of course, is what comes of marrying a Swede. 'Even a turnip, let alone a Swede, would know not to bury its other half on a day that clashed with Home Park,' Tommy Moor-Bodmin remarked with his usual incisive wit, 'but there's no way out. We shall have to do the honours. Bloody shame. We could just as easily have laid the old bugger to rest on Monday.' Each of the guns, as was their wont, drew a number. One to four acted as pallbearers, five to eight as ushers moving up two. At the start of the service Percy the head keeper blew a blast on his horn to let the vicar know it was time to drive the choir into their pews.

"The coffin was a great sight draped all over as it was in four by two and surmounted by crossed cleaning rods. Furthermore the vicar was in excellent form. Getting on a bit, is the vicar. Tends to stray off the line sometimes and get names slightly wrong. At one point in his address he remarked that: 'The Stiff we know and love is gone and yet he is still with us.' Which was in a way profoundly true. The stiff was right in front of him in the coffin.

"The vicar, the Reverend Septimus Sponge-Knightly, was himself a great shooting man who never refused an invitation from his hospitable parishioners, even if it was only single guns. He took as his text '*God sees every sparrow that falls to the ground.*' But not, he stressed 'every pheasant, partridge, duck, grouse, woodcock, ptarmigan, wildfowl, capercaillie or snipe. Otherwise the good Lord would never so specifically have nominated sparrows as a protected species.' It went down very well. Several of the beaters applauded and Colonel Wildbore-Slaughter made a mental note that he must propose Septimus as Honorary Chaplain to the Game Conservancy.

"After lusty singing of *Onward Christian Soldiers* and *Happy Birds who Sing and Fly around Thine Altar, oh Most High*, the congregation, Barbour-clad to a man, woman and dog, adjourned to the open air.

"The eight guns ranged themselves on either side of the grave. They mounted their weapons. Three salvoes rang out. The bag was a brace of pigeons and a jay which fell rather neatly on the coffin. The not unattractive keeper's wife choked back a tear as she beat Ursula by a whisker to cast the first clod, scoring a bulls-eye on the jay. It was an excellent wake. The sloe gin flowed as if there was no tomorrow, which alas, for Stiffy, there wasn't, or do I mean was? They made the best of it and did Home Park in the afternoon. Stiffy would have wanted it that way."

Our hero paused so that Frothy might have the privilege of paying for another round. "A few nights later," he announced in confidential tones, "I had a rather odd dream. It was that while the guns were busy doing Home Park, Stiffy was presenting himself at the pearly gates. St Peter eyed him quizzically, jangling his keys the meantime. 'This,' he said, 'is the moment when you look back through your life and recount your transgressions.'

"Stiffy paused to reflect. He pitied poor Cecil when his time came. All those low birds and claiming twenty-seven when he knew damn well he had only potted nineteen. Not a hope for him. He could think of three or four other guns who would probably be done for poaching, and then there was Freddie who made a hobby of swinging through the line, but what had he, Stiffy, ever done wrong? He really could not imagine.

"'Your Saintliness,' he said at length. 'I have to confess that I am at a loss. Of course, one has one's off days. One cannot always be on song. One does occasionally under-tip the keeper if the gee-gees have not been behaving properly. One has been known to consume more than one's share of tomato sandwiches at the shoot tea, but otherwise ... ', he shrugged his shoulders.

"'Well,' said St Peter, 'you had better come in, on a trial basis – both ways. After all you may not like it up here. There are no Purdeys and no birdies, but you can still have days when you are on song. You can put your name down for the heavenly choir. Do you happen to know the words of *All Things Bright and Beautiful, All Creatures Great and Small?*'

"Stiffy stood it for almost a year and then asked for a posting. In the meantime, passing the time of day with St Peter, he had let slip the nature of the activity in which he had been indulging at the moment of his untimely demise. This just may have been why he suddenly found himself back on earth in a rabbit warren. He lolloped along the tunnel, made his way towards the daylight and cast an eye around. The coast seemed clear and it was sunny. He felt peckish. He went in search of greenery. The terrain seemed vaguely familiar. In fact, on closer inspection it became extremely familiar. He was in Home Park. Cocking a furry ear he could hear the jolly sound of the beaters moving in line towards him, accompanied by a bevy of spaniels, labradors and retrievers.

" between you, me and the gatepost, Peter — I've had a few low birds and under tipped the odd keeper..."

He moved ahead of them at a positively hare-like pace, so that he might station himself at a point of vantage and get a good view of the sport.

"There were the guns, waiting by their pegs. He looked for Cecil, Freddie and the others. None of the familiar faces was to be seen. Instead he found himself gazing at a bunch of weirdly attired individuals, many of them sporting silly moustaches, one of whom was busy missing a seagull while another was blasting away at a chaffinch.

" 'Great Heavens,' said Stiffy to himself, 'this is a let day. And to Italians, no less. I trust they are aware that the rule is no ground game.' At that moment a large individual, who appeared to be a cross between Mussolini and Pavarotti, caught sight of him. Stiffy only just made it behind a hillock in time. He could hear the shot thudding into the ground some distance away. He spent the remainder of the drive behind the hillock. The standard of shooting, he concluded, was nothing short of deplorable. On his way back to the warren he came face to face with the not unattractive keeper's wife who, on her return home, could not wait to tell her husband of the extraordinary behaviour of a rabbit she had come across in Home Park."

He who Brings Comfort to those Bereaved by Death or Divorce

Terence Toy-Boy, like your average politician, is not in the habit of staying in hotels at his own expense. He does not, on the other hand, consider a visit to the Big A to be tolerable, let alone enjoyable, if his modest means dictate that he must stay in some sleaze pit on 42nd Street, between sheets with cigarette burns and with murders taking place every hour on the hour down the corridor. A suite at the Carlyle is more his style. In Hong Kong the

Mandarin, in Cape Town the Nelly (Mount Nelson to outsiders), in Venice the Chippers (the Cipriani to the non *cognoscenti*), on Dartmoor Gidders, in the New Forest Chewton Glen – one could go on. How then to maintain reasonable standards of comfort when the wanderlust strikes?

He realised long ago that nothing is for nothing. As the *maître d'* said at the Connaught, "There is no such thing as a free lunch."

E'er he reached his prime, while he was yet in his salad days, Terence, then an attractive brunette, without a grey hair to his temples, would lie in his bath, a glass of Bollinger in his small but perfectly formed hand, waiting for the sun to attain the yard-arm and considering the problem. Attractive young women expected you to pay for them. He could not quite think why, but they did. Unfortunately he did not feel drawn towards ageing loaded gays wanting their money's worth. "Bottoms up" was a jolly toast but not, for him personally, an inspiring thought.

What then did that leave? It hit him in a blinding flash, causing him to put down his loofah and cease persecuting his plastic duck. Very rich, elderly, divorced or widowed women. Lonely women. Insecure women who do not wish to be mugged, raped or robbed. Old plastic ducks who like to be fawned over, lied to about their beauty and generally cherished. But ducks who had reached an age when they also cherish their nocturnal privacy.

Ever since, our friend has made a point of cultivating all diamond-encrusted miracles of survival that venture into his magnetic field. This may on occasion entail turning a frozen shoulder on an infinitely more appetising specimen of the deadlier sex. He has even, on occasion, in order to seek out promising material, invested in a cruise. He has even gone so far as to learn various archaic dances such as the quickstep.

He has indeed paid the price. He has also brought home the biscuit. "Why, Mrs Clara Belle Hickenlooper the Third. I think a week at the Crillon to take in the Arc de Triomphe would be a most lovely idea. How very gracious of you to ask me along.

Why, I have not set foot in the Crillon since the Windsors had me over for the opera." (Terence does not consider such harmless embellishments to be mortal in their sinfulness.)

"My dear Contessa, I would not hear of you going to the Bar au Lac alone. You know how crazy I am about playing bezique. Shall I bring my mah jong set in case we feel like a change? Next week is quite free (certainly so far as I am concerned)."

"Dear Lady Spendeasy, will we be taking the helicopter or the Ferrari? Gleneagles is so relaxing. Maybe after dinner we can discuss your will?"

As Terence is wont to observe, where there is a will there is a way.

Willie B. Chauvinist is taken out to Lunch by his Bank Manager

Nowadays, of course, one's bank manager can turn out to be a woman. Should Willie be invited to lunch by his bank manager and shown into the bank manager's office only to discover a neatly suited female with a brisk haircut opposite him, he will at once say, "Good morning, I have come to have lunch with the manager. Will you kindly let him know I am here? Say that again. Did I hear you say you are not the manager's secretary? Are you trying to tell me in your discerning feminine way that you are the bank manager? By jove, there's a turn-up for the book. Carrying she-who-must-be-obeyed into the work-place, what? First the priesthood, and now banking. I hope you won't mind my saying this, but the fair sex do have a bit of a reputation for tittle-tattle. I would not want my daily to know how my account is doing any more than I would want the Chancellor to know too much about my offshore trust. OK, you keep your own counsel. I trust that does not mean – ha, ha – that you are supporting a penniless barrister. As if I would rub you up the wrong way. Delectable as you are with those huge come-hither eyes. The right way maybe. That was a harmless jest. I expect you girls rather like a bit of sexual harassment from time to time. Quite flattering really. Penalty of gate-crashing a man's world. I do hope you don't want me to put you up for Boodles.

"Now what happens if you suddenly have great expectations? Who is left holding the baby. Your husband or the deputy manager?

"So far as the day-to-day running of my affairs is concerned I would hope you would take an avuncular, or in your case aunt-like, interest in my financial activities. Look on yourself as my sleeping partner. That's another harmless jest, by the way.

"And if you ring me up and I am over my limit and you pretend to be fearfully cross, will you warn me if you are not really cross but just suffering from a touch of PMT?

"Of course you must have some time to go before the old change. But you will warn me when it starts? And tell me if you are on HRT, won't you? No need to if by that time you have moved to the main board although I would always be delighted to be kept abreast of your news. There I go again."

Willie's eyes naturally fall upon the uplifting contours of her Wonderbra surmounted by a cleavage that reminds him of skiing off-piste at St Moritz. He contemplates leaping across the desk in order to cement their blossoming relationship. Maybe he should content himself with an increase in his limit and a reduction in rate to one over base.

"Well," he announces, taking care not to ogle her so long that her ego might over-inflate. "I think that my overdraft is safe in your beautifully manicured hands. Let us to lunch. I shall just have to steel myself when the bill arrives. I shall feel, mind you, like a kept man. In fact, bearing in mind the sinfulness of usury, you might almost call it living off immoral earnings.

"After you, dear lady, or should I say manageress?"

"Bloody odd being treated to a slap up lunch by a sexy little bank manageress with excellent legs – hope you won't be expecting me to put you up for Boodles..."

"Well," stammers the host, "I just thought perhaps we should. Good form and all that. Show willing, what?" The guest, in this case Leonard Lingerwell, whose family have farmed at Chauvinist Court for generations, is both puzzled and shocked. Many is the Sheraton three-pillar dining table that carries a burn or two from Leonard's meerschaum as a memento of interminable post-prandial chit-chat. Even when the smoke from his pipe has made it all but impossible to breathe, let alone catch the eye of he who is sitting across the table, Lennie remains rooted to his chair.

"Shall we," pleads the host, injecting a note of supplication into his tone, for he knows how his dominant mate will react to the chaps lingering over their port (it will be more S than M when bedtime comes), "join the ladies?"

"Why?" innocently asks Leonard. "Are they incapable of having an interesting conversation on their own? Can't they have a lesbian love-in for a little longer? Give them an inch, mark my words, they will make our lives hell. Next they will want to come with us when we go to Thailand." Leonard's point is so sound that within a trice another bottle of Taylor's '45 is grudgingly placed on the table. Even though the prudent host had acquired it at Berry Brothers in 1948 he is not unaware of what it is now making at Christie's. No good sending any up to the drawing room. Someone has to drive home. Anyway they would not appreciate it.

Despite intermittent thumping noises on the ceiling, they have a thoroughly enjoyable chat about women, their disabilities, idiosyncrasies and general inferiority. Leonard does not pull his punches where women are concerned but has a great deal of time for them in their proper place. Bed, the kitchen, the laundry room, the supermarket and the school run.

He does not consider it their place to be in the Garrick, or, except after parties, in the driving seat literally or metaphorically. Should the men, out of the sheer goodness of their hearts, an hour and three-quarters having elapsed in the twinkling of an eye, be so tremendously unselfish as to join the ladies, Leonard will lead the way so as to steal the credit for this act of charity.

He ushers his host's little flock into the salon. "Ah ha, there you are, I trust we have not kept you waiting." (Brilliant, any troubled waters are instantly calm.) A bevy of grateful members of the weaker sex beam up at him. "Of course not. We have been having such a fascinating chat, haven't we, Cynthia?" Cynthia, who has never got a word in all evening, fails again. "Not been watching a video then?" Leonard breaks in cheerily. "No, I bet not. Been concentrating on girlie matters I dare say." "Certainly not. We have been having a very serious talk about politics." "Just as well we did not rush up in that case."

And so, thanks to Lennie, everyone is completely happy. Cynthia goes down to make some more coffee for the men and does a bit of clearing up while the percolator is reheating the Nescafé. Our hero meanwhile laments the lack of black-tie dinner parties nowadays. "One used to dress properly so as not to let down the staff. Now half the men don't wear ties and if you hire staff for the evening they all roll up in dinner jackets. Quite recently a friend of mine answered the door. He showed the first arrivals into the garden and gave them a glass of champagne. Found out they were both students and knew his son. Only when he reminded them that he had not specified black tie did they manage to tell him they had been hired as waiters. Jolly difficult nowadays.

"Must be trolling along. A wonderful evening and I did so enjoy the beef. Lamb, was it? Well, anyway it was jolly good. And the crème brûlée. Brûlée's the word, eh! Anyone going in the direction of St John's Wood? Well, that's awfully good of you. I say, is that not a tiny bit out of your way if you are heading for Dorking? Actually it won't take you too long to get back on the road if you take the M25."

The Case of the Straight Lothario

Another feature of Leonard's flawless character is that he has a soft spot for penniless young men of good family setting out to do the Season, involving, as this wholesome activity does, a minimum of seven invitations a week throughout the entire summer, in fact, these days, most of the year. The time is long gone when Lolitas are only in season when oysters are out. If only they, the young bloods, damp behind and no doubt between the lugholes, could go in to bat even with a soupçon of that mastery acquired by our hero over the years.

"So, dear boy. You are about to delight debutantes. Oh, to have your vitality and my expertise. As you cannot lend me the one, I shall have to impart to you as much as I can of the other. You do of course suffer from two disadvantages. You are penniless and you are ignorant of the ways of the world. Being penniless is of no consequence. Just as small men are always falling in love with and marrying huge women – that is nature at work righting the balance – so youths with empty pockets are forever becoming besotted by girls of great wealth. Once again that is nature.

"I have often been tempted to become a backer – an angel to use the theatrical term – of an insolvent young male of pleasant appearance in return for a modest cut of the fortunate young female's fortune. A sort of financial Cyrano. I buy the dinner jacket, the Charbonnel and Walker, the Raybans. I even defray the cost of the weekend for two at Le Touquet where you, what is, I believe, nowadays known as, "do the business", immediately prior to popping the question.

"Now how can I make you a trifle more cogniscent of the ways of the world? You must, for a start, obtain admittance to the boudoir of a past mistress of the arts of the bed-chamber. The Duchess of Windsor being alas no longer with us, and you know who being jealously guarded by her theatrical scribbler, you will just have to make do with Kay Y. Knott – an ageing but vibrant female who makes Joan Collins look out of sorts. You should suspend an apple from the ceiling and exercise your tongue by pushing it for a minimum of one and a half hours per day.

"Pity you went to Eton. Wykehamists have such lovely manners. Still, never mind. Back to your heiress. Do your best. Admire whatever appalling outfit she turns up in. Compliment her on her orthodontist. Make a pass at her mother. I am sure, if you just imagine you are a cross between the late Alan Clark and me, she will be Blu-Tack in your roving hands."

Charles Bovey-Tracy and Dressing the Part

Rule one. Whatever the state of the wardrobe, the sensitive guest must arrive with an appropriate number of suitcases. Carry-on luggage is an insult to one's host.

Supposing he omitted to pack his Gap DJ and Garrick cummerbund? He obviously would not dream of offending his host by enquiring whether this would be the correct rig for dinner. On arriving thus attired in the drawing room on the Friday night at the appropriate hour, only to discover his fellow guests to be kitted out in moth-eaten pullovers, he does not turn a carefully pomaded hair. "Forgive me," he murmurs, "I thought you mentioned dinner. I did not realise you meant supper. I will just pop up and change into something a whit less formal." A whit indeed; he returns having slipped into an immaculate green velvet smoking jacket.

By the following night he has enthusiastically entered into the spirit of the thing. He skips merrily in, sporting trainers, jeans and a perfectly frightful khaki sweater with pads on the shoulders. How was he to know that every big-wig in the county from the

"... Forgive me, I thought you mentioned dinner – I didn't realise you meant supper – I'll pop up and change into something a bit less formal..."

Lord Chancellor to the Lord Lieutenant had been summoned and that he would be surrounded by a school of penguins? Never mind, his *savoir-faire* will see him through. Better to be under-dressed than overdressed.

Due to the vagaries of the British climate, dressing is a tricky business. Furthermore, who can say what one's host has in store for one? It is all too easy to get caught on the hop, even on the briefest weekend stop.

Not only might there be, in the event of careless packing, considerable loss of face. The situation could easily become life-threatening.

Just supposing Charles B-T is invited down to Wiltshire by one of his jet-set, airline-owning friends and has not seen fit to pack either wading stick or crampons? His friend is not jet-set for nothing. His pride and joy is his Cessna. The runway starts just beyond the kitchen garden.

By lunchtime on the Saturday Charles may equally easily find himself half way up the north face of the Eiger or, for want of a wading stick, floating gracefully down the fastest flowing river in Scotland, namely the Spey, towards Fochabers and the open sea. Full mountaineering kit, plus waders, seventeen-foot rod, fishing bag etc. are a total must.

Our guest has not been so forward as to enquire whether they are taking in Ascot. Indeed he has not ascertained whether there is any racing at Ascot – but to be caught with one's morning dress pants down would be sartorially unthinkable.

Supposing, that while he was in Scotland fishing, come the evening the party adjourned to a Caledonian ball? One cannot be too careful. In goes kilt, glengarry, skean-dhu, sporran, the full kit.

His letter of invitation contained no mention of a fancy-dress ball. But you never know with the Kesdales. Any more than you do with the Lanwicks. Better pop in the Marie Antoinette outfit to be on the safe side.

Say there is an all-star charity cricket match in aid of the local home for retired antique dealers. And, say, Gary Lineker lets them down at the last minute and, say, he is asked to fill the breach. Whites, pads, trusty old bat, Garrick cricket cap, box. Better safe than sorry.

He gets it all in the Volvo. No problem. He would be lost, mind you, without a roof rack.

⤝ As You Are Up ⤞

As the devilishly charming guest sank back into his favourite chair at the Garrick, his acolyte Frothy Fotheringham continued to hang on his every word.

Meantime he continued to hang onto the 1962 Hine, thoughtfully provided by the said Frothy.

"I don't know whether you have ever come across the Boodle-Plouveries?" He did know. Frothy hadn't.

"Pity. A weekend at the B-P's is not lightly to be refused. Hermione always takes Anthony Worrall-Thompson to bed with her and as a result gives birth to some noble nosh. What with her husband Sebag's cellar being awash with first growths and the bedrooms being irreproachable, one goes around humming 'could one ask for anything more?' Just the place for R&R and bags of TLC.

"One's fellow guests are normally on a par with the bedrooms.

"Finding myself undernourished to the point of malnutrition a week or two back, no fellow gourmet having had the good taste to ask me to Nico at Ninety or even the Connaught, I contacted Hermione and gave her the good news that I was free that weekend. Excellent brandy this, Frothy. Top it up if you insist.

"Down I totter – it would not be over-egging the pudding to say I was looking forward to a square meal. Even a round one would not have come amiss.

"In through the portals I barge, only to be rooted to the spot, transfixed with horror and disbelief.

"There in the hall, as small as life and three times as nasty, hovers George Grovel. May I take it that you, Frothy, have led a sheltered life and have never endured a country house weekend in the company of George?" Frothy nodded.

"George," the good guest continued, "is that most irritating of all mortals, the Helpful Type! He is what hostesses refer to as 'a joy to have in the house' who 'won't let you lift a finger' and who 'you really miss when he's gone' and so forth. You know the sort. Rushes out to the kitchen and brings in the *dauphinois*. Tries to look manly by scorning oven gloves. Scalds himself – pretends he hasn't.

"That the Georges of this world behave like this is solely because the good God, by an oversight, has omitted to endow them with any of the airs and graces of polite society. They are not easy on the eye. They dress abominably. Never having been Dean of Westminster Abbey or Foreign Secretary they have nothing of interest to contribute to the conversation. As likely as not they do not even play the pianoforte.

"Did they not devote every conscious minute to butling, gardening and drink-pouring, gushing like a geyser the while, no sane hostess would contemplate having such a poltroon – nerd if you prefer – under her roof for an instant.

"The trouble of course is that if one is not frightfully careful, George and his like will, while one is attempting to emulate the lilies of the field, make himself *persona* extremely *grata*, be pronounced indispensable and be invited down incessantly, to the horror even of the staff who do not take to being made to look, and even feel, redundant.

"So it was that I expressed my misgivings to one Angela Tight-Bottom, a highly sexed, comely – forgive the repetition – fellow guest over a pre-prandial tipple.

"Talking of tipple, Frothy. This Hine is, as I am proving, quite drinkable. Well, just one more.

"as this is proving quite drinkable - I'll have one more..."

"Angela agreed something must be done. But what? Suffocate
Hermione's peke and slip it under George's pillow? As pekes go it
was less unpleasant than many and, apart from a touch of slobber
on one's shoe, had never done either of us any serious harm.

"There had to be a better way.

"We decided to enlist the help of a third party – Cynthia
Smartarse, fresh from Girton and with a first in applied biology.
As you would expect, Cynthia was no sludge when it came to
game plans. 'I think,' she announced, 'this is a proper case for
bringing into play the AS YOU'RE UP gambit.'

"Come dinner and there, as was his wont, was George holding
Hermione's seat as she sat down (Hermione would rather he had
contented himself with holding her chair), unfolding the double
damask and spreading it unctuously over the most intimate parts
of her anatomy and generally being his habitual nauseating self.

"Angela took it upon herself to open the bowling. 'George,'
she called out with a resistance-melting smile, 'as you're up. I

left my Raybans in my room. Top floor, second on the left. I do find candlelight such a strain on the eyes. Would you be an angel?'

"'And,' added Cynthia, 'while you are up there would you bring down my Dupont. It's on the bedside table, beside my vibrator. Don't try to stroke Klaus. Pit bulls are very territorial. He regards my bedroom as his patch.'

"'Certainly,' said the odious George, 'no problem.' Wrong, of course. Klaus bit him. 'Not to worry,' said the unspeakable George. 'Had a tetanus jab last year.' What a damn shame, I thought.

"He was in the process of lowering his Elastoplasted rear onto his Sheraton shield back when I decided it was my shout.

"'George, old thing. As you're up. I have a feeling I left my binoculars at the end of the garden near the magnolias. Just beyond the nettles. The rain can't be doing them much good. Take a torch if I was you.' I may say that I was thankful that I was not.

"Meanwhile, Angela, Cynthia and I were making a pretty good fist of bringing in the *soupe de poisson*, handing round the *croûtons* and dishing out the – or to be more precise *le* – Montrachet.

"When George, sodden from the rain and still exuding blood from the trousers of his M&S pin-stripe, returned, having wasted ten minutes in a fruitless hunt for the non-existent binoculars, Angela flashed him a smile which brooked no refusal and wondered if, as he was up, he could bear to give her au pair a bell and make sure she was catering to her live-in partner's every need.

"And when George finally attained a sedentary position the *soupe* was not even *tiède* and the *croûtons* had all but disintegrated along with the *rouille*.

"Throughout the repast, whenever George was in danger of relaxing or making a move towards the cruet, one of us instantly conceived some fulfilling errand; adjusting the Sky dish on the roof perhaps or rescuing the cat from a tree. (Silly me, it's a bird's nest. I could have sworn it was a moggie.)

"'As you're up' in due course became interpreted as 'as you're

"...as you're up, would you be an angel?..."

the one nearest the door/light switch/window/lavatory/what else?/garage' (crash). It was all hugely satisfying.

"Come lunch the following day what was left of George seemed to be attached to his seat by a magnet; positively clamped to it. Never made the slightest effort to be any help at all. Sat there, a beaten man, mumbling 'please pass the pepper'.

"'Rather off George,' Hermione announced – George having very kindly popped out to the village garage to check up on my tyre pressures – 'he used to be such a help around the place.'

"I sympathised, 'He does seem to take you a bit for granted nowadays. Perhaps you should rest him for a while, if you get my drift.'

"She nodded.

"(Well, why not, Frothy? A small one, same as the last.)"

⚊ *Aide Memoire* ⚊

"Dear Boy,

"Adrian and I are delighted you can be with us on New Year's Eve. We shall be twelve. The dress is cardies. As you are the only non-locals I thought it might be helpful if I put you in the picture as we see the old out and the new in.

"Talking about seeing the old out, I trust that Wilfred lasts the evening. He used to hit the bottle, but of late the bottle has been having its revenge. On no account mention the army. Something to do with mess funds. He has just been passed over – talking of which, no jokes about the Passover either. Hiemie and Rebecca are both – well, you know – but even so, absolutely charming. And he's done awfully well. Slightly anaemic meat but first rate cellar. Archie and I would not want to upset them. Claud, he's the tall one, is Kim Philby's nephew. Could you bear to keep off traitors? Oh, and drugs. I forgot to mention that Wilfred's daughter is in a clinic.

"Now, you may not find this easy, but can you manage to get through the evening without getting on to cricket? Rebecca took her dear little Sealyham Flossie to watch the village play Potters Bar. Bert, our head gardener, hit a massive six right on to poor Flossie. Rebecca bursts into tears at the slightest reference to our national sport. Try not to use phrases such as 'I was completely stumped' or 'I was absolutely bowled over'. Incidentally, Bert went on to make a century and we won by six wickets.

"Vital – do not allude to Newbury – or any other bypass. Julian has had three in the last ten years, none of which seem to have worked.

"Jennifer Polkington, who you might have met with us at the Game Fair – and my goodness isn't she just? – will be having an egg. Could you bear to let this go by without comment? She is allergic to everything except eggs, lemon barley water and men. You may, by the by, get the impression that she is winking at you. This is a congenital twitch. If however you feel her hand on your thigh during dinner this could be better news. I am told her restricted diet in no way impairs her sub-duvet performance.

"If I may revert to Julian for a moment. His daughter is somewhat pregnant by a Rastafarian who happens to be an extremely talented oboist and who is currently appearing in the Park Lane underpass. Please therefore do not make witty asides about blacks, single mothers or those who play wind instruments. (A word or two about the charming ambience of the Park Lane underpass would not, however, go amiss.)

"Should someone feel the need to pop out to the powder room in the course of the evening please do not greet them on their return with 'Ah! Ha! you've come out of the closet then.'

"Cecil just has. He and Glenda are carrying on together notwithstanding the picker-up that Cecil picked up while shooting and whom he has now installed, most appropriately, in the folly at the bottom of the garden. Glenda, not to be outdone, has taken up mud wrestling. Quite a few things to steer clear of there.

"Annie (subject to Jennifer, see above) will be yours for the evening. Absolutely straight-down-the-line normal girl. Feel totally free to talk to her about anything you like. Anything under the sun except loo paper. It's a long story I will not weary you with.

"I did not, by the way, invite the Crepuscula-Harflytes – there's far too much chance of being invited back.

"That's about dealt with everyone except you – don't worry, I have warned the others not to raise the subject of television licences – and the two of us, Adrian and I, I am happy to say, have no skeletons in our cupboard, i.e. we buried his parents at sea, which is why we can afford to push the boat out on the 31st.

"See you then,

"Irma"

"No, darling – I can't invite the Crepuscula-Harflytes – there's far too much risk of being invited back..."

Guestmanship and Politics

"The floating voter," as Bertie Floorcross is wont to observe, "makes democracy possible. No, my party, right or wrong, has never been for me." He finds this sentiment both laudable and totally convenient. Atop this high moral plane he is in a position to castigate all those who vote Conservative as:

1. Slavishly following in their parents' footsteps.
2. Doing so because they think being Tory is socially smarter.
3. Interested only in their personal financial welfare rather than in the welfare of the country.

Those, on the other hand, who vote Labour he perceives to be:

1. Intent on surrendering our sovereignty to Brussels.
2. Full of reds under the bed, wolves in sheep's clothing, etc.
3. Far too soft on gays.

We now come to the Liberal Democrats. Bertie has a great deal of time for the Lib Dems. He likes the cut of their gib. Never likely to govern. Lot to be said for PR. Nice, earnest, fair-minded people who can stand on the touchline throwing biodegradable missiles at both sides (in a constructive way of course). Pity they are so passionate about Europe.

Having said which, there are occasions when he will argue passionately for closer integration with the European Union. Bertie is a man of moods. Should he find himself breaking bread with a bunch of Little Englanders he will not hesitate to come out with such helpful remarks as, "Mark my words, if we don't join up for the common currency in one or two years at the latest we are finished. Done for."

Or, "Some of these regulations coming out of Brussels are really very sensible. All trafficators to be on the right of the steering wheel. Excellent. At the moment if you are driving a strange car you are quite likely to turn on the headlights every time you wish to turn right."

Nothing is more galling to anti-marketeers than the suggestion that Brussels knows best. Except perhaps, "Good fellow, Neil Kinnock, very sound. Excellent brain." That really gets 'em.

Bertie, however, does not dine solely with those who, though they might not say it, would not lose too much sleep if one atom bomb fell on Brussels and another on Strasbourg, so long as the wind was blowing in the right direction.

No, he casts a wide net and rates culinary excellence and a good claret as the main reasons for accepting an invitation. Other guests at the party who keep a good table and might produce their diaries before the end of the evening are a bonus. The politics of the company are there to provide a source of merriment.

Having ascertained that all of those present have progeny at Eton, Winchester, Wycombe Abbey or Heathfield he will in-evitably jump on one of his most time-worn but stimulating hobby horses. "I see another six boys have been threatened with expulsion for peddling heroin. Makes a change from sodomy, I suppose. I don't know, bearing in mind that most of the masters join in, and most Labour MPs are gay and proud of it, why it is still looked on with disfavour. Sir Charles – Charles if you insist – aren't you a governor of one of those outdated establishments where one pays five figures a year for seven years to buy an accent? Do fill us all in about what goes on, always supposing they tell you anything. Or is it all a closely guarded secret, like the Masons? Forgive me, I forgot you were a grand master. But then I am not really meant to know, am I?"

Having dealt with the public schools the good guest will, as likely as not, home in on the monarchy. If he has discovered before they sat down that the aunt of one of the wives has a great friend who happens to be (happens to be, a cut above just being) a lady of the bedchamber, then nothing will deflect him from his purpose.

"You can say what you like about the rest of them," says the

"Aren't you a governor of one of these outdated establishments who one pays five figures a year for seven years to buy oneself an accent?..."

ANNIE TEMPEST © 2000

wife, "but HM has done a wonderful job." With a deeply pained look on his face, Bertie feels compelled to allude to the striking similarity of one of the offspring to a certain earl. "I would not," he intones gravely, "mention such a thing if I did not know it to be true. I would not dream of promoting unsubstantiated tittle-tattle." He has a great deal more unsubstantiated tittle-tattle up his sleeve to be conjured up in due course. He concludes by proposing the immediate abolition of the monarchy. "In my view this should all be set out in the next Queen's speech at the same time as proposals for the confiscation of the public schools, the disestablishment of the Church of England, the re-introduction of National Service and of course the noose."

"Oh! Goodness me! I forgot you were a Grand Master —
but then I'm not supposed to know that, am I?..."

Bertie concedes that this does not exactly coincide with Liberal Democrat policy, but then he has always prided himself on being a floating voter.

When it comes to politicians themselves, his correctness is of the essence. Clearly New Labour will see out not only this millennium but doubtless the next as well. The hellish guest, having taken this sobering fact on board, has dismissed all his Tory parliamentary friends as meaningless irrelevancies, faded relics from the past, shadow foreign secretaries of their former selves.

Those who once bathed in the reflected glory of having sat two places from Portillo at dinner must now move on. The brass plaque commemorating the evening when John Gummer graced Bertie's reproduction Hepplewhite dining chair has now been tastefully removed, to be replaced with a photograph of Charles Kennedy.

Bertie, not unmindful of Scottish omnipresence on Labour's front bench, has been working on introducing a suspicion of a Scottish brogue into his previously carefully cultivated, impeccable accent.

Though unlikely to govern, might the Lib Dems be going places? Ming being such good value and Charles such an eligible, if trifle overweight, bachelor, they make excellent dinner-party fodder – particularly since they, unlike the Tories, are *persona grata* on Cabinet Committees.

Why Bertie Never Stood for Parliament

Elected to serve. Tea on the Terrace.
Drinks in the Members' bar.
Who knows indeed? One day perhaps
Official car.

Send in green card. He will be thrilled.

Picking up boards like pins.
Putting down lots of questions
Along with double gins.

Finding causes. Acquiring strong views
And expertise
Soon when he catches a cold his
Leader will sneeze.

Bright future. Toe the official line.
The Whips' favourite.
"Nice speech" says the Chancellor.
Savour it.

The years pass by. Back-bencher
Bored by inaction.
Make them sit up. Become
Part of the faction.

Bane of the Whips. Maverick.
Votes for no motion
He does not believe in.
Adios promotion.

No special K. No happy day
Of visiting the Palace.
Farewell to all ambition
Welcome to malice.

Master and Man

Angus McSporran had as an infant received much character-forming instruction at the knee of his splendidly middle-class

Scottish grandmother. "Always keep a bar between master and man," she had exhorted him.

Initially he had taken this advice to heart and in his youth had always insisted on calling all retainers by their surnames. He did not retain such retainers for any length of time, due to a slightly overdone tendency to keep tabs on their industry and honesty. "Had to sack Kelly. Counted the new potatoes. Two short." Nor did Flanagan survive after Angus discovered that he was paying her for two hours and quite often she only did one hour and fifty-five minutes. As she worked tirelessly during the time she was there he might have turned a blind eye, but for his shrewd suspicion that she had made a telephone call to her sick mother in Donegal while he was sunning himself in Morocco. (Frightful place. Water switched off at night. Endless flies. No papers. *Times* crossword, obituaries etc. vital to relaxation. Virtual certainty of contracting African tummy. Regular thunderstorms. Three changes of planes. Ten hours by air door-to-door.)

As Angus eased himself into early middle age, however, his approach softened. As he perfected his technique of maximising the number of days in the year when he could live at other people's expense he concluded that the success or failure of an entire stay often depends on the rapport established between guest and staff. "He's such a lovely man. Nothing is too much trouble where he is concerned. A real gent. Not like some of these jumped-up, too-big-for-their-boots types who like nothing better than to lord it over you. If he told me to go jump in the lake I'd do it for him. Strewth I would." Or, of course, in the case of attractive tweenies, into bed.

From time to time Angus is invited to stay in a feudal castle in a far-flung corner of the realm. His train arrives late in the evening. He is met by the estate manager Plodworthy, thankfully not in some naff top-of-the-range Range Rover but the vintage, almost pre-Phylloxera family Rolls. It will take them some forty minutes at a steady 38 mph to reach their destination. What a cracking chance for a good chat. Does he consider he is underpaid? Will he be allowed to remain in his tied cottage after retirement? Will his Lordship continue to pay his heating bills, car insurance, telephone and so on? What sort of pension has his Lordship in mind? How many years has he been in his present position? How many weeks holiday is he allowed? Can unused days be carried forward from year to year? In short, are his considerable talents, his efficient performance in a position of responsibility and his (careful of that cyclist) unswerving loyalty both appreciated and properly rewarded?

Prior to this watershed of a journey Plodworthy has been wholly content with his lot. His wife, mind you, has been on at him for some time, but he has heretofore dismissed her misgivings as groundless. "Don't you go worrying your pretty little head; we are very well looked after." Now he cannot count the minutes until he is with her again. "I think there might be something in what you say, my dear. I shall ask for a word with his Lordship after the weekend."

And so, before he is even within the battlements, Angus has forged a close alliance with he who holds sway over the estate. The word will go forth. Angus's merest whim is to be instantly gratified. They, the staff, have among them a true gentleman, deeply concerned for the welfare of those less privileged than he. By the time Angus takes his leave, he has, with a quiet word here and a discreet comment there, encouraged them to form a union. In the evening, as the Union Jack is lowered from the flagpole atop the east tower, those below stairs assemble for a spirited rendition of *The Red Flag*.

"Damn funny business," his Lordship is heard to say the next day, "Bofers, head keeper, y'know, just told me that brother McGregor was off-colour and won't be beating today. Never realised the fellow was a monk."

Never does anything by half measures, does Angus. A great believer in the cutting-edge.

The Elderly Vehicular Guest Holds
Forth on the World as it is Today

The country is being run by unsound whippersnappers, many of whom live in houses full of bought furniture. Take this unleaded petrol nonsense. I had my Bentley converted and before you could say John Prescott it was stalling its head off. And, although I never actually kept a check, I just knew, in the way one does if one has been about for a bit, that I was doing fewer miles to the gallon. Government rip-off as usual. We were all perfectly happy for years and years with leaded petrol. I shall have the old girl put back on the proper stuff at the earliest opportunity.

Of course, personally I am old enough to remember when every Tom, Dick and Harry did not own a car. Now your school leaver on the dole, male or female, drives a Porsche. People were a damn sight happier, if you ask me, in the old days. The lower orders went by bus or bicycle and were all the fitter for it. If they were that interested in driving there was nothing to stop them becoming chauffeurs.

As for safety belts. I have had mine taken out. Absolute menace. Most uncomfortable. If I wish to injure myself it is my inalienable right as a British citizen and a member of BUPA so to do. If my passengers do not take the same view they need not accept the hospitality of my car. Speaking of which, I have a cocktail cabinet attached to the back seat and have no hesitation in stopping on the hard shoulder, if I happen to be driving along the motorway at an appropriate hour such as noon or 6pm, for my usual tipple. I do, and I mean this, drive rather better after a few drinks. The adrenalin flows.

These speed limits on motorways are quite ridiculous. In fact, I take the view that they cause more accidents than they prevent. I believe that in certain European countries those who drive bigger cars are allowed to drive faster than those who drive little cars. Quite right too. If someone of substance wishes to purchase an expensive car one may take it that he may have urgent appointments with other men of substance.

I well remember the late Sir Malcolm Hilberry, a judge of the High Court and a freemason, saying to me, "People with fifty-mile-an-hour minds should drive at fifty miles an hour whereas those with one-hundred-mile-an-hour minds should be allowed to drive at one hundred miles an hour." I do the ton, as I believe it is nowadays referred to, without compunction. It is good for the engine. Blows the cobwebs away.

I may be an elderly buffer in the eyes of the younger generation but I certainly am no fogey when it comes to new inventions. For example, I thoroughly approve of automatic gearboxes. To have to change gear manually with one hand, while holding one's car telephone in the other, would, I imagine, be downright danger-ous. I thought this woman Margaret Thatcher was going to set us free. Yet, in spite of all these years of having had to endure the humiliation of being led by a female, we are still hemmed about by restrictions. Nanny says this, nanny says that, nanny says your tyres need replacing. Nanny says it is time you had your MOT. Nanny says you must not cross a double white line. Where, if I may make so bold, will it all end? George Orwell never warned us about Big Sister. Typical woman driver if you ask me. Indicates she's turning right and damn well takes us down the same old socialist road of pettifogging petticoat government. And now we have this milk sop of a successor Mr What's-his-name Blair. Just as bad as that woman, if not worse.

What gets my goat almost more than anything else is the atti-tude of the police to parking. Why do they not go off and clamp a few muggers and buggers? I will tell you. Because they are almost to a man, and I dare say woman, bent. Do you let the police know if you are going away? I certainly do not. No, they draw their backhanders from hardened criminals as a thank-you for informa-tion received and give vent to their sadistic desires by penalising innocent folk like yours truly for double parking in Park Lane during the rush hour. Let's face it. A chap has to park some-where. He must not offend his host. Good manners are the first consideration. *Noblesse oblige*.

Our Hero Extends the
Hand of Friendship to Fellow
Members of the Commonwealth

Down Under and hell are of course one and the same thing, but into everybody's life an Australian must occasionally fall. Our hero is particularly good with Australians. He takes the view that the fact that they are Australian is in no way a fault of their own. They were born that way. Theirs was not a domicile of choice. They are not to blame for the crimes of their forebears. Had their forebears not been transported as an alternative to the gallows they, and the rather endearing chips on their shoulders, would not exist. Our hero realises that they owe their appalling accents to the necessity of speaking with their mouths closed during the incessant sandstorms and bushfires. He cannot, for the life of him, understand why the excellent notion of exporting our most dangerous criminals to this outpost of the Commonwealth has been discontinued.

He is actually a great admirer of Australia and quite often serves its amusing little wines at his less important dinner parties. He has a Sidney Nolan print hanging in his cupboard behind the coats. He holds Australia in such high regard that but for the geni-talia boasted by his Jack Russell he might have called him Matilda.

Whenever he finds himself dining with an Australian he bends over backwards to put him or her at his or her ease. "Tell me," he enquires, beaming with avuncular goodwill as if his Abbo guest had flown in specially from Broken Hill instead of having come from Earls Court in a mini-cab, "what does koala taste of? Eucalyptus? Do you boil them up in a goolagong? And you must help me out with my geography. Do you come to Australia before or after India?" He then goes on to praise great Australian singers such as Nellie Melba and Kiri Te Kanawa. "You say Kiri Te Kanawa hails from New Zealand? Same thing. Antipodean."

"The one thing one must never do with these people is to patronise them," he is wont to say. "I tend to tell them how fascinating it must be to eke out one's days in such blissful solitude – away from all the hurly-burly of the civilised world. After all, most of them have television, and from time to time there are excellent documentaries produced about Venice and Florence and the Alhambra and the National Gallery, all of which are doubtless shown on Aussie TV within a year or three of our seeing them. Splendid surf riding of course – as long as you know how to cope with sharks and skin cancer. I suppose if you live in Tasmania, Sydney must seem quite cosmopolitan, what with its bridge and its opera house. Interesting architecture – looks as though it's been put up specially – if you know what I mean. I like these self-made countries. I really do. Very colourful. Especially the parrots. And the immigrants. I must say I do long to see the outback. It is, I imagine, much like Essex."

Our hero is very fond of the old song that goes

My great great great great grandpapa
Was a man who murdered his wife
So they sent him to Australia
For the rest of his worthless life
He lived down among the trees
With the Aborigines
Now the family is well born
Yes its quite the best in Melbourne.

He forgets how it goes on. Anyway, good on them. Sport.

..."Must be fascinating ekeing your days out in the blissful solitude of Australia away from all the hurly-burly of the civilised world..."

The Guest's Expatriate Friend

He was something very senior
Out in Kenya,
Before they brought him back to Tunbridge Wells.
I think he was in jute
Or he may have been in fruit
Before they brought him back to Tunbridge Wells.

He earned the commendation
Of the nation;
He did forty years apart from leave in spells.
He might have been in tea.
He rose to number three
But all the while he longed for Tunbridge Wells.

He said to me "I've been here
"Out in Kenya
"For forty years with cheetahs and gazelles
"But I cannot stand the heat
"So I'm beating a retreat
"They are going to bring me back to Tunbridge Wells."

Alas it is a coffin
He's flown off in
Sound the bugle for the saddest of farewells.
He's in teak as four strong men
Bear him airborne home again
To his last retirement home in Tunbridge Wells.

The Guest and the Gracious
Transpondite Hostess

Jonathan Bull always keeps his visits to New York a closely guarded secret. Air India. False beard. Turban in Garrick club colours. "There is," he is wont to say to his pal Frothy, "nothing in this whole wide world more totally unspeakable, more utterly intolerable, than your New York society hostess. With the exception of the Duponts, the Mellons, the Rockefellers and a very limited number of other families, there is no such thing as gentry to be found in all America. Even they, of course, are by European standards possessors of money so new that the ink on the greenbacks is barely dry. As for aristocracy, now Mrs Simpson is no longer with us ... but there we are. Thus, in an interminable but hopeless quest after gentility they give these fearful parties, feeling no doubt that if they rub shoulders even for a brief evening with an Englishman their lives might be enhanced and with luck the merest whiff of class might rub off on them.

"In these circs one would think that these transpondite *arrivistes* would pull out every stop for one; ashtrays everywhere, a table groaning with vast quantities of butter, decent wholesome foods, i.e. meat with plenty of fat on, bags of cream with the pumpkin pie and so on. Not a bit of it. The husband works out every morning at the New York Athletic Club then jogs back across Central Park, still managing to hit Wall Street somewhat earlier than a civilised man would contemplate easing his pins on to dry land from his water bed.

"His wife, a liposuctioned beanpole, has long since banned smoking, eating and drinking from the apartment. If an Englishman wishes to seek out that sort of hospitality then, my dear Frothy, he has only to stay in this country and repair to Champneys. I would not be one whit surprised to hear that some of the stick insects that prowl Park Avenue had been run over by a feather. Indeed, I am convinced that deaths from malnutrition among the hyper-rich food faddists must be legion. I cannot think why they do not all become astronauts, what with their being so accustomed to weightlessness.

"I would have a meal first and then join them for the conversation, but for the fact that their cocktail hour starts just after I have finished lunch and by late teatime they are already rounding off their non-event of an evening meal pecking at a decaffeinated coffee sorbet. So eating beforehand is out. As one is ejected at ten fifteen or so one can then try and right the balance by returning to one's humble pad to fry up a few slices of *foie gras* and quaff a bottle of Yquem, always supposing that one's already dormant host has been thoughtful enough to leave his wine cellar unlocked.

"Anyway, the conversation at these self-denying get-togethers tends to be on a par with the nosh – one wonders which particular lettuce leaf of a thought one's neighbour might wish to toy with. The best route to Martha's Vineyard? Armani's sale? Am I going to the benefit at the Met? It would most certainly benefit the soul of said neighbour if she ever paused, while actually attending such events, to look at some of the exhibits instead of wafting her jewel-encrusted frame round the museum, clutching her glass of Perrier, attempting to spray regal charm on all and sundry and concentrating on the only sort of eating she indulges in – that is to say man-eating; in other words making an exhibit of herself."

— *The Guest from Hell Offshore* —

"I will tell you," Billy West-Meon said one evening to his pal Frothy as he opened the Moët and Chandon his tailor had given him as a hint his bill was yellowing at the edges, "why I tend to decline offers of hospitality from my dear sister Audrey in

Guernsey. It arises from an interesting fact, calculated to shock even the most lukewarm canineophile. There is only one beach in the entire Bailiwick where dogs are made welcome during the summer months. From every other strip of sand – our furry little friends are banned."

Guernsey being outside the European Union, this flagrant breach of a dog owner's rights to take his pooch with him to whichever public place he may wish to repair to cannot be tested in the Courts.

This is, of course, an outrage, particularly as it costs a paw and a leg to fly one dog from Gatwick to Guernsey and back again. Were children under the age of fifteen also only allowed on one particular beach, and certainly not that one on which dogs are permitted, then dog owners might not feel quite so hard done by. The trouble is that children and dogs regard beaches as fulfilling different needs. Toddlers like their Daddies to hit tennis balls in the air, so that they and their Daddies may both make fatuous attempts at catching them. Woofers feel it their duty to join in, frequently carrying the ball off to the other end of the beach and burying it.

There is nothing an infant enjoys more than to attempt to eat one of those concoctions made from whipped-up pig fat and that for some strange reason are called ice-creams. Some dogs, to their lasting shame, have such undiscriminating palates that they insist on helping out. It may be, of course, that in their loving and helpful way (their only wish is to please) they seek to benefit the health of their young chums by removing those odious offerings from their diet. There is one particular problem caused by the concatenation of juvenile and man's best friend which demon-strates beyond all doubt that the Bailiff of Guernsey and his henchmen would be much wiser to introduce a form of apartheid, so that while one beach would echo to the yaps of poodles and growls of mastiffs, others would be rendered even less peaceful by the cacophony that emanates from the immature.

What is that particular problem? The innocent beachcombers lie somnolent. They have partaken of an excellent picnic; their miniature schnauzers of a quantity of digestive biscuits washed down with Evian water. No sooner are the beachcombers dreaming happily of hiring some pied piper to cajole every noisy offspring into the sea (no waterwings allowed) than they are rudely awakened by an outraged mother.

"Your dog has just committed an offence on my child's sandcastle." What to say? Lead off a spirited discussion about property rights on public beaches? "When you refer to a sandcastle as your child's would you enlighten me as to why, simply because he has wasted the entire afternoon building it, instead of learning his seven times table, he now owns the freehold?"

One could, of course, exercise one's right of way and proceed to walk right over it, flattening it. Or one could try the conciliatory approach. "He was only trying to help. He thought the moat was screaming out for a golden stream."

In the event that the offence committed turns out to be of a more major variety, all is not lost. Go over and inspect the little lad's work and point out that your dog's offering looks jolly realistic – just like little cannon balls.

The problem, of course, would never arise if the, no doubt spoilt, brat had not been allowed on to the beach in the first place. This would have left Hubert and Humphrey, Bill's miniature schnauzers, free to concentrate on courting couples. They have it down to a fine art. She lies in her bikini, her eyes closed, waiting. Her lover's eager lips move close to hers. His deft hand caresses her firm breast. At that moment Humphrey licks her left ear, while Hubert nibbles her big toe. It never fails.

— *Barging In* —

Percival Lootless is the most reasonable of men. When it comes to holiday invitations he realises that not all his friends can afford to pay for him at places like Sandy Lane, the £8,000 a week joint in the West Indies so beloved of the pathetically rich Michael Winner. Indeed, there are hosts so strapped that even a sojourn at the modestly priced Gazelle d'Or would be beyond them, particularly if they are throwing in his air ticket.

Thus, when the Broke-Phuckets asked him to join them for a week on a barge belonging to their friend and patron Charles (not down to his last) Sandwich, Perce, after much cognition, during which time he heard nothing from Michael Winner and not a squeak out of Sir Don Gosling, decided to accept.

Perce makes a habit of cultivating useful people. Thus it came about that his old buddy Garth Rees, for years West Wales welterweight lifting champion, considered it an honour to drive his suave hero and his luggage in a barge-ward direction on the appointed day.

Garth effortlessly lifted the fitted trunk and deposited it on one of the bunks in the master-cabin together with the fax, rowing machine, exercise bicycle, Dobbie – Percy's Dobermann – oil skins, filing-cabinet, waders and much else including those crystallised fruits of which he was so inordinately fond and which he made a habit of presenting to his grateful hostess immediately prior to devouring them himself.

"Welcome aboard," intoned Charlie B-P, just a soupçon of a frown crossing his impoverished face as he tried to pick his way over Percy's packages.

"Am I," enquired Perce, "correct in recalling that the front of the boat is known as port and the rear as starboard?" He had assured Charlie, when his joining them was discussed, that messing about in boats had been his lifelong passion. He did not however intend that this expertise afloat should result in such unthinkable horrors as him being asked to pull his weight. One must, however, look willing. "Swing the tiller to aft when you want to go for'ard. Use the bow thrust to go faster. It may take a day or two to get the hang of it, but not to worry. One can't come to much harm at four knots, can one?" "Allow me," insisted Perce as he wrenched the lump hammer from Charlie and proceeded to conduct a savage attack upon a mooring spike – so savage in fact that this vital piece of equipment bounced out of his lifeless hand to be lost in the murky depths of the canal. Irrepressibly cheery as ever he beamed at a desperate Charlie and continued, "Not to worry. As likely as not the old ham sandwich will not even notice it has gone."

"Time I took a turn," Perce remarked shortly after they had set off, "at the helm. A man's job, don't you know. No room for Tiller girls on board, eh?" With which jocular quip he assumed command and scraped the barge all along one side as he attempted to go under a bridge. "She seems to have a mind of her own," he murmured as what was left of the boat emerged from under the bridge only to ram the side of a moored barge, holing her just below the water-line. He could see Charlie needed cheering up. "That's just the sort of prang insurance companies are for." So saying he slapped Charlie on the back thereby pro-jecting him into the canal. "Maybe you had better steer the old girl for a bit. Help you dry out. Mind you, I felt I was getting on top of things. Still, if you want to hog the driving, go ahead. I am a guest, after all. I'll just concentrate on the cooking from now on."

It was only a small fire. A roll of cling-film which Perce had left beside one of the burners on the oven, which set light to the washing-up cloth Perce had left beside the cling-film. If only the tin of lighter-fuel had not been on the towel… Anyway, Perce was wonderful. It was under control in no time. The fish pie had a bit of a funny taste, which could have been the powder from the fire extinguisher. All was well in the end. A touch of singeing here and there.

After that, Perce concentrated on decanting the wine and watching television. The third night they decided to patronise the local pub. Perce assumed that in view of his munificent largesse in the form of the crystallised fruits – he had much enjoyed them – he would not be required to put his hand into his borrowed RORC blazer for wallet-extraction purposes. Just to be on the safe side he left his wallet behind with Dobbie.

"Wonderfully restful holiday," Perce remarked to his host as Garth was removing his few bits and pieces from the barge. "Dobbie, say thank you for that leg of lamb." Dobbie growled in appreciation and Mrs Broke-Phucket dropped six plates.

⤙ *A B & B from Fred Freeby* ⤚

"My dear Chris and Jennifer,

"I must say that I and my numerous party all thoroughly enjoyed our all too brief stay in your newly acquired lovely holiday home in Gascony.

"What a tragedy that you could not join us. We have already taken the liberty of recommending it to a number of our more spirited friends. You really should have charged us something. Being very conscious of your generosity we left various partly consumed goodies (butter, jam, croissants, prawns etc.) in the fridge by way of a modest thank-you. I trust you will be there before too long.

"You are so wonderfully generous to let every oddball ride roughshod over your pride and joy. I don't mean us of course. We went out of our way to leave the place in even better shape than we found it. Incidentally, our French came on apace while we were there. *Par example* (for example) I do hope you approve of our rearrangement of the dining-room table and chairs and the ping-pong table in the garage. By interposing them we have at a stroke created an intimate and unusual dining-room on the one hand and a really luxurious games room on the other. Just wait till you see.

"Had the idea occurred to you of putting the three new white sofas from the living room round the pool? They looked terrific and, mark my words, will again when they dry out and someone gets rid of the grass stains.

"*Je pense que* (I think that) you will, when next here, be hugely appreciative of the murals executed by the young who came with us. Those large areas of bare wall, which, if I may say so, erred on the side of minimalist, were screaming out for that wonderful freshness of vision the pre-pubescent bring to their creative activities. How sexually precocious they are nowadays. If you ever have anyone fragrant to stay, you could cover the offending wall with a rug.

"Let us move on to the subject of telephones. Yet again I left my BT credit card behind. When we arrived, the young, who are very good about that sort of thing, asked if it was OK to get on the blower. I said I was sure, you being no sludge, that the tab was picked up by your company, so feel free. They regarded this as a great boon and only wished you had had two lines. What with Jamie trying to finish the *Times* jumbo crossword with the help of his pal in Cape Town while Ian (the tall one) was queuing up to ring his Peruvian number who was back home visiting her parents, they almost came to blows.

"Had huge fun studying your photograph album – I wonder if you will agree with our comments. Douglas has indeed aged dreadfully. Is he ever likely to look at the album? I don't know who wrote that particular comment. It could have been me. We did get through a fair amount of the alc – we felt it all looked so pitifully undrunk. You were well out of some of the champagne – presents from undiscriminating friends no doubt – the Veuve Cliquot was OK. We found the Giscours '90 very closed up. Maybe we should have let it stay that way. The Grand-Larose '83. *Excellent.* Almost up to the '82. Pity you only had one case.

"*Par la rue* (by the way). We did not immediately come upon the instruction book, but from the moment we did so (two days before we left) not another coffee ground went down the sink and nor did we take any more of the best glasses to the pool – not that many of them were still in one piece by then. My late brother-in-law always swam in gym-shoes – a frightfully wise precaution in my view.

"In the confident hope that this can be an annual event the young have put in a lot of work on the pot plants, i.e. they have turned over just under a hectare of land round the pool to marijuana. This meant sacrificing the lavender and the young poplars; a small price to pay if you ask me. By this time next year we should have quite a decent harvest. Do feel free to nick some. It is after all your land. You should also have a fine showing of poppies in due course. I love poppies, don't you?

"You will also find a small supply of speed (Keith to his friends – joke) at the back of the medicine cabinet, this is a small thank-you from all of us to you two for all your kindnesses.

"It never ceases to amaze me the way the mistral appears from nowhere. Doubtless you know someone who can repair or replace the umbrellas. Had it not been an act of God (I am an agnostic myself) I would certainly have insisted on paying for the damage. Surely there is a way of letting them down at night?

"And now (*et maintenant* – yes, the old frog is coming on apace), a heartfelt apology. You know the book of instructions I was talking about – the file with "Guard This With Your Life And Be Sure To Leave It For Your Successors" in heavy caps on the front?

"We, and you will think that I am joking (would that I were) inadvertently slipped this splendid tome into the old Honda when abandoning ship.

"Taking it shortly we were at one of those *aires* having a picnic – in fact tucking into the last of your *foie gras* – only the *canard* but never mind – when Matilda wanted to check up on whether we should have left any tips for the staff. She then propped it against a tree. After we set sail I said, "Are you sure you did not leave it propped against that tree?" and of course she had. We were a bit behind schedule – we wanted to make Paris by six to have plenty of time for the old pre-prandial tipple – so we decided (by a majority vote) against going back for it. Sorry about that. The good news is that at least the coinage in the plastic case where you show £1=10 francs etc. (which of course it doesn't) was not wasted. We ran short of change one day.

"Did we mention that Howard, our American guest, won the prize for the fastest speed up the track? We paid the farmer a modest sum for his dog – it was only a mongrel.

"We did manage to get rid of Michel, the *soi-disant* (so-called) gardener, for you. He started tu-toiing Matilda so I sacked him. Thin end of the wedge. Anyway, his trousers were a disgrace.

"We broke a *cafetière* but have ordered a new one. Be sure to take 105 francs when you collect it. They cost more in England by the way.

"In general you said in the instructions – it was the *aire des adieus* by the way, fancy my suddenly remembering – to let you know if anything is missing so you can 'keep numbers up'. I enclose a list. I also enclose a list of odds and ends removed in error, such as the brass wall-sconce in your bedroom.

"*En passant* (in passing) we came across one of the best restaurants in the middle of nowhere. Just fell on it, doesn't figure in any of your Goat Millyers. Fabulous food and drink. Absolutely sensational. Mouth watering. Superb house wine at 35 francs a litre. For nothing. We meant to collect a brochure and slip it in the file. Lucky we didn't as we lost the file. It might have been called the Auberge de Something. Or it might not. Anyway I am sure you will come on it. Not to be missed.

"It is quite rare nowadays to find everyone in a house party smokes. I always say that a house should not just feel lived in, but smoked in. Yours now does. I would have asked Michel to remove some of the stubs from the gravel, but see above. Our comments in the visitors' book (couldn't our predecessors think of anything to say?) were totally sincere, especially Daisy's. 'Great to be somewhere where Dad does not go ballistic every time I leave a light on.'

"Must stop. Hugely grateful. Unforgettable.

"*Même temps prochaine année?* (same time next year)

"Yours aye,

"Your perfect guest,

"Fred Freeby

"PS. Talking of smoking, you know what they say – there's no smoke without fire. The east bedroom in the loft needs a new fire extinguisher.

"PPS. A leg on one of the deck-chairs broke due to a design fault. They should cater for big men like Ian. Suggest you complain to the manufacturers.

"PPPS. I once wrote a rather amusing poem.

"How I wish I could afford
To spend the rest of life abroad
But if I did, eventually
Abroad would be at home to me."

⚊ *A Holiday Beside the Infanti-side* ⚊

Harri I. Hatim has nothing against children *per se*. Indeed, he once experienced the shortcomings of immaturity himself.

Mindful of this he is perfectly willing to put up with them for short periods, providing that they are impeccably behaved and ruled with a rod of iron by a stern father who grudges every penny he spends on them. Their mother should be someone whose prayers for infertility fell on deaf Almighty ears – thereby proving that God is a left-footer. The children's parents should also have taken the precaution of acquiring a fit nanny, who should make a point of escorting them to bed at an early hour, using only such force as is reasonably necessary – e.g. dragging them there by their left ear.

On no account should any children be allowed to attend any holiday at which Harry is present until they have outgrown acne, orthodontics and all the other disfigurements of adolescence.

He has a particular allergy to any child in the process of shedding its milk teeth. Such under-sized ogres should, in his view, instantly be despatched to Pony Camp the moment their Mummy and Daddy contemplate foreign travel.

Harry is not much given to nightmares. He usually manages to while away those happy hours he spends between the sheets reclining on his goose-feather-filled pillows dreaming of first growth clarets, sirloin on the bone and Naomi Campbell.

On one occasion however ...

He has just arrived in some sub-tropical Shangri-La. Among his fellow guests are an American couple. She, riddled with guilt that she has continued with her career after unwillingly giving birth, he entering into an early dotage and putty in the hands of their daughter Anthea, whom they have, of course, brought with them.

Of course? Yes, of course. They take her everywhere – when they go out to dinner, away for the weekend, to bed, to the loo, to confirmation, to the dentist, to the golf course, to the colonic irrigation clinic, to hospital for a D&C. Wherever. Anthea is right in there with them. They like her to feel involved.

This egocentric tearaway, with her constant demands for attention, her whining reiteration of the words "I want", her refusal to allow any conversation to take place which she does not both instigate and dominate, is in danger of seriously interfering with the harmless pleasure of her elders and infinitely betters.

The sleeping are woken, tennis is abandoned in mid-set, bridge in mid-rubber. She is particularly insufferable at meals, being totally unable to taste, let alone swallow, any food that is even remotely un-American. Even more wearing than her dietary requirements are the evenings, which are devoted entirely to admiring her total lack of artistic talent.

Harry considers the easy way out, i.e. getting up, but, deciding to persist, after his customary 4am excursion, he lies down and takes up the thread once more.

Not for him, he decides, the locking of the bedroom door, the plugging of the ears and a prayer that the time will pass quickly. He is of sterner stuff.

"The candy in the fridge is mine," announces the sepulchral Anthea, hands on hips as she addresses the assembled party, "and none of you are to touch it without my permission, which will, by the way, be refused." Harry carefully injects each bar with a powerful emetic. Anthea is a sturdy girl. Later in life it will be written of her by a swain:

Our love cannot wilt
Our romance cannot curdle
You are heavily built
With a wide pelvic girdle.

Her recovery is much too quick. Something more dramatic needs to be done.

Chancing upon Anthea's mother by the pool, looking ravishing in her Bloomingdales's one-piece, he addresses her. "Trust you do not mind my mentioning ... Anthea charming ... promise ... not ... betray ... confidence ... no ... objection ... corporal punishment ... within reason ... even for girls of her age ... little shocked ... severity of your husband's chastisement. Really did look as if ... trying to hurt her. I remonstrated ... naturally. Have a look ... bruise ... left arm ... if I was you."

He had seen Anthea collide with a door, thereby creating an unsightly contusion just above her elbow. The outcome, Anthea's parents being of the transatlantic persuasion, is never in doubt. The threatened divorce. The suggestion that in such an eventuality the husband's money will be dissipated on his wife's lawyers' efforts to persuade the court that this tyrant should never set eyes on his daughter again. Were he other than an American odd-ball he would grab her arm off at such an attractive offer.

As it is he takes himself off to the pool in his New York Athletic Club Bermuda shorts to contemplate the injustice of life. Harry joins him. He feels honour-bound to tell him about how he has come upon the houseboy and Anthea's mother ... must promise not to divulge source ... never came across that way of doing it before ... I doubt even in *Kama Sutra* ... unexpurgated version."

They leave the next day. Just before Harry wakes up. As he is wont to observe, "Even nightmares should have happy endings."

The trouble is that dreams do have a nasty habit of coming true. Not long after the aforementioned nocturnal experience, Harry joined a houseparty at Villa des Poufs, situated at the very epicentre of the Côte des Ponces, for what was supposed to be an all-male, screamingly witty, if the conversation flags, hand round a joint, ten days. Harry, though himself of the boringly straight persuasion, does find an occasional break from doing his duty and satisfying the needs of every heterosexual female within range a most restful experience. A good book, a glass of wine and no thou beside him in the wilderness does not, from time to time, so that the batteries might be recharged, come amiss. He does, it should be mentioned in passing, find lesbians hugely attractive. But that is another tale, not relevant to the present proceedings. Immediately had our hero, who had honoured this occasion with a mauve cravat and some particularly pungent aftershave, broached the portals, he sensed that some best-laid plan of wasp-waisted man had ganged most fearfully agley. Feet were being stamped. Falsettos were hitting high C. Two Sheridans were having tantrums. Cecil Smallbottom was perilously near to going into one of his declines. His host, Ambrose Pushkin (known to his intimate circle as Princess Pushy), was quite definitely having a conniption-fit.

"Do I detect, my having an instinct for these things, that all is not well in the nest?" he asked the weeping princess.

Ambrose looked at him in misery. Clearly more that his wrist was cracking. "We were going to have such a truly wonderful time. I had it all planned. Excuse-me dances. Sardines. Cross-dressing competitions and much," he gave our hero a meaningful look, "more. Then Cecil meets this American at a party. Not just any old party. Bunny's thrash of the year. Cecil had gone as chief whip. Anyway, Cecil was having one terrific time with a camp-as-all-get-out American who said his name was Harvey Wallbanger. So he invited him down here. He said he knew I wouldn't mind. 'Do come and bring a partner,' he said. 'Great,' said this guy, 'and may I also bring a small encumbrance?' Well, of course, Cecil had no idea what he was talking about. He thought it might be a strait-jacket, or perhaps just handcuffs. 'No problem,' he told him.

"No problem," screamed the princess. "No sodding problem. Harvey, whose real name is Clint, turns out to be a bisexual schizophrenic. He has arrived with Hilary, his wife from hell, and a twelve-year-old in tracks from somewhere infinitely worse. You only have to look at her from afar to realise that her hobby is breaking down bedroom doors and shouting 'Got you!' What are we going to do?

"We have tried all lighting up our Dunhills during dinner and that almost worked but not quite. They went off for a walk in the grounds and there was a thunderstorm. We have had frogs' legs beautifully cooked in garlic by our ravishing young chef and unpasteurised cheese and although they have not eaten a thing for days they seem determined to stay the course. Can you help?"

If Harry had not had his nightmare he would not have known what to do.

THE PAIN OF THE RAIN IN SPAIN

They told us, so it's churlish to complain,
That "the rain in Spain stays mainly on the plain".
We got soaked on our siesta
We got drenched at the fiesta.
And a heavy dew put out our barbecue.
I doubt the weather's fairer
Higher up in the Sierra
So it's us and not the sky that's feeling blue.
If we go and see Granada
Will it rain but even harder
Than the rain in Spain that stays upon the plain?

Shall we shelter with our camera
While it pours on the Alhambra?
We very well may not come back again.
Our day trip to Marbella
Was under an umbrella
And would the Spanish Tourist Board explain,
How it happens that the Costa
del Sol is an imposter
And when the rain in Spain will start to wane?

How the Guest from Hell Copes with the Rain in Spain

1. Blame the weather on the owner of your small hotel.

2. Do not rush some of the simpler tasks. For example, have you lost your comb? Put off finding it until after breakfast. This will give you something to look forward to (apart from the end of the holiday).

3. Try a series of sarcastic remarks on the owner of your small hotel. Here is an example: "Autumn is very beautiful in Spain." If it is mid-July your irony will not be lost on him.

4. Invent some fun games. Here is an example. Collect all the dirty washing and put it in a pile by the bidet. Then sort out a pile which would do one more day and put it back in the wardrobe. Reconsider the matter.

5. Ask the owner of your small hotel whether in his opinion any improvement in the weather may be expected in the next day or two.

6. Get some more stamps and postcards. A misery shared is a misery halved.

7. Read a good book. Then re-read it. Or even better, read it aloud.

8. Take your time in the lavatory. When the hand trying the door handle becomes really desperate call out, "shan't be long," and start another chapter.

9. Be an optimist. Nothing is more annoying in all life than someone who insists, despite the forecast, that it is about to clear up.

10. Play cricket in your Pak-a-mac. This will amuse the Spanish.

11. Ask the owner of your small hotel what you should do all day.

12. Develop a cold. (Keep the family in touch with its progress,

with phrases such as "it's thickening up nicely", "sort of greenish" and so on).

13. Grow a moustache.
14. Smoke more. This will give you a more interesting cold.
15. Drink more. This will help you sleep.
16. Eat more. This should have a bearing on number eight above.
17. Telephone home. The weather in England is wonderful. Your pleasure is complete.
18. Make a special calendar which shows how many hours, minutes etc. it is until you go home. Show it to the owner of your small hotel.
19. Sit down. Pick up your pen. Think of nineteen ways in which you can make a wet holiday in Spain more fun.

The Young Female Guest Seeks a "Position" on a Yacht

First insertion
English stewardess (twenty-seven) seeks post on large yacht. Happy disposition. Zealous. Decorative. Bilingual.

Second insertion
Licensed English stewardess. Warm. Very friendly. Photo available. Just the right age. Has had French lessons. Great stamina. Bisexual.

Third insertion
Licentious, ravishing English stewardess, at the height of her powers, seeks interesting position on large yacht. Very friendly indeed. Own bunk not necessary. Can turn hand to anything. Insatiable.

Fourth insertion
Ravishable, topless English stewardess, 36-24-36. Seeks fulfilling post on large yacht. Likes nothing better than to be hard at it round the clock. Very experienced. Will look after all kinds of passengers and crew. References available from satisfied customers. French lessons a speciality. Over the age of consent.

Fifth insertion
Dominant English stewardess wishes to keep order on large yacht. Pumps iron. Pumps anything. Very stern. Black belt in constant use. In bond. Suit marquis.

Sixth and final insertion
English stewardess seeks post on yacht, large or small. Works well in a team. Likes to do things in groups. Open to any suggestions. All ages.

The Perpetual Guest,
Believe it or Not, at Home

The perpetual guest is a martyr to his friends. He goes to them. Were he an old stick-in-the-mud, did he not consider it tasteless to flash his money around, he would remain at home and insist that they come to him. But that would be alien to his noble character.

Would he find getting stuck into the clearing up, after they had at last taken their leave, a burden? Of course not. He finds the emptying of ashtrays into the compacter, the carrying of empty bottles into a receptacle so that they may be conveyed to the bottle bank, the putting into the dishwasher of half-empty glasses containing his best wine, a therapeutic exercise – a thoroughly rewarding experience.

No, no. He regards it as an honour for his benefactors to cross his threshold. He does, of course, regard those who are concerned with whose turn it is to have who with the utmost contempt. Squalid is the word that springs to his fertile mind. He is, however, so fully occupied accepting other people's invitations that he rarely has time to do any entertaining of his own. And he is, of course, a bachelor. Bachelors never ask anyone back.

Nevertheless, just occasionally, he feels that a reciprocal gesture is called for. The day dawns when he realises that those who have incessantly invited him to the Helmsdale, Covent Garden, the West Indies or whatever, are beginning to feel they are being taken for granted. That would never do.

It therefore comes about – albeit on occasions of the utmost rarity – that he plays host to some of those who have had the good fortune, nay the honour, of treating him.

The meal, thanks to Sainsbury's and his microwave, is no problem. He nips through the Eurotunnel to Calais for Tesco's excellent Vins de Pays D'Oc at £1.50 or so. There is only one problem. So rare an experience as being entertained by the perpetual guest is not something that those so privileged would wish to bring to a premature conclusion. How then does this doyen of the social round rid himself of those he has allowed to interlope, at a reasonable hour?

Over the years he has amassed a series of gambits for achieving this end. If one does not work the next one might. They are:

1. Dammit, my watch has stopped. Has anyone got the time?
2. Your driver must be freezing. Shall I invite him in for a cup of tea?
3. Have I never shown you my video of Diana's funeral?
4. How about charades? It's only midnight.
5. Don't even contemplate getting your second wind. Your first was quite bad enough.
6. I am afraid you can't use the loo. I have just switched on the burglar alarm.

"How about Charades – it's only midnight!.."

7. At this time of night one can speak one's mind. I fancy your wife rotten.

8. What? No one has ever taught you bridge? We will have the table up in a jiffy. Who cares if the moon is over the yard-arm?

9. You don't have a dish? You have never seen *Neighbours* in German? Step this way.

10. It is noon in Sydney. Just a thought.

11. That must be your mini-cab now. Forgive me, I thought I heard you ring for one.

12. One for the road? Advocaat?

13. If you would rather not drive we can certainly put you up, so long as you can both squeeze into Freddy's sleeping bag. The poor incontinent soul is away at school.

14. Back in a flash. Just nipping into my dressing gown.

"At this time of night one can speak one's mind –
I rather fancy your wife…"

15. The central heating is on a time switch. Would anyone like a pullover?
16. Join hands everyone. "Should auld acquaintance ..."

— *Time to Say Goodnight* —

Your ordinary run-of-the-mill guest fades inconspicuously away. He completely fails to break up the party and as likely as not his departure goes totally unrecorded.

This will never do for our friend. No, no, no. He starts saying, "I must not be too, too long" at about twenty to ten. He fills the party in on his movements the following day. Not too precise of course. "Pretty early start. Stop off in Abu Dhabi. Lunch with the Sultan. Then on to a very tricky business meeting with the Albanian Minister of Transport."

Should he bump into his host in Harrods next morning he will be ready to describe in graphic detail the fog or sandstorm that has closed the airport.

He does not, of course, leave at twenty to ten. From that moment on, however, he earns Brownie points for each extra minute he remains. He incessantly looks at his watch but clearly finds the subject of conversation, namely leasehold enfranchisement, so absorbing that he cannot bear to tear himself away.

Midnight strikes. He is rooted to his chair. One guest is yawning his head off. His host is audibly somnolent. He is such a brick to stay on that none of the others would dream of making their escape. They are trapped. Having changed the topic to "what I would do if I were Prime Minister" the guest from the nether regions is in fact rapidly getting into his stride.

"I do believe," he announces, "that – do pass the brandy would you – I am getting my second wind. I may have to go direct to the airport." From then on he never draws breath. Not for a moment. One cannot leave a party while someone is in full flood. At 2am

"It's noon in Australia.- just a thought...

he suddenly exclaims, "My goodness, just look at the time. Sadly I must be on my way. I have thoroughly enjoyed listening to you all."

Even then he is not done. He proceeds to stand astride the threshold summarising all that has been said. He even threatens to go on a Cook's tour of the house. Eventually he moves towards the car. The rest of the party are now in a very parlous condition.

"I'd better make a move," he announces. "I'm blocking you all in." He finds that he has mislaid the car keys. After an interesting crawl under the table of the dining room, which had been candlelit and is now in darkness, they turn up. He tries to start the car. The other guests are quickly on hand with jump leads. By the time he gets going they are, for the rain is now torrential, soaked to the skin. He waves them a cheery goodnight and is gone, having made a lasting impression.

A Welcome Guest

The bogs and the mist and the cold united to prove, to any inmate yet to be convinced, that Dartmoor was an inescapable fact. At about midday a diminutive figure on a motor scooter shot down the hill and pulled up, more by luck than good judgement, outside the main gates. He rang the bell. There was the traditional clanking and eventually a sodden, rusting, bad-tempered screw asked the visitor, mixing his language more than somewhat, what he wanted.

"I won't have that filthy talk," said the little man.

"You won't, won't you?" bellowed the warder, limbering up.

"No, I won't," the tiny scooterist replied, "I happen to be the new Governor."

The warder humoured him. "Quite, sir, and my name is Mick Jagger. Nice to have you on board." He was just about to say, "Now beat it," and fling him a few yards into the courtyard when

"If you'd rather not drive, we can certainly put you up as long as you can both squeeze into our grandson's sleeping bag - the poor incontinent soul won't be using it tonight..."

he remembered a mucker of his saying that the new man was half-litre-sized. He let him in.

The new arrival beamed at his senior staff as they sat around the room tucking into his sister's fruitcake.

"So," he went on, "I want my ship to be a happy ship. I want to brush up our image. Here we are in this idyllic setting in one of nature's beauty spots. We must make this a prison that men vie with each other to be sent to. Now let's look around, shall we?"

The head warden, Mr Slughem, walked with the new man. "We really must have more flowers about," said the latter as they proceeded. "Flowers do cheer a room up so, don't you think? I shall get one of those nice young girls to come in twice a week on a contract basis.

"And now let's look around," went on the Governor, "on this first tour I want to be spared nothing, but nothing."

They had now reached the lavatories. The Governor was shocked. He stood surveying matters in stunned silence for a full two minutes. "But this will never do," he murmured at last, "it simply isn't on."

"Isn't on what, sir?" Mr Slughem was puzzled. The pans and urinals had been brought to a high state of polish in honour of the inspection. The brass gleamed like gold – even the graffiti had been touched up where necessary.

"For one thing," replied the Governor, "you have no choice of paper. That nasty hard stuff with OHMS on it is totally unacceptable. Let us offer those in our care something more gentle on the skin and, what is more, in prettier colours." Mr Slughem's bull-neck tightened and his eyes started forward in their sockets.

"And how about frilly covers for the lavatory seats, sir?" he grated.

"Excellent, excellent – I have an aunt who makes them to give away at Christmas. I will put her to work – make a note. And then we shall want those little bottles you hang in the cistern that make the water in the pans a lovely Mediterranean blue, which turns of course to an enchanting green when in use. With tufted rugs and pretty curtains the whole area will be transformed. We cannot have any 'Ballads of Reading Gaol' written here, can we, Mr Slughem? Now, onwards, onwards. What have we here?"

"Men's recreation room, sir."

"Oh, no, no, no, Mr Slughem, no, no, no." He looked round despairingly. "I mean the decor. Oh, dear, dear. Make a note, will you. Write down: Mr Parr of Colefax & Fowler to advise on scheme using soft pastel colours. This is a neo-Georgian building, Mr Slughem. We must bring out the best in it, must we not?"

"And now let's meet the men."

"Good idea, sir, they should be in from the working parties anytime now."

"Who are those people attired in those disgusting battle dresses?" The Governor, small though he was, was beginning to sound quite cross and intimidating.

"Inmates, sir. Them's inmates."

"Make a note, Mr Slughem. Bruce Oldfield has a country house not too far away, you know – ask him to get a design out. We want our chaps to be a credit to us, don't we, Mr Slughem?"

"Yes indeed, sir, by all means, sir," Mr Slughem winced.

The Governor called the first returning party to a stop and approached it.

"I," he began, "am your new Governor." He put out a hand to the first. "How do you do. My name is Pipplewick."

"Pull the other one," came the reply from Smokey Sefton – a hit man from Bermondsey noted for his rebellious attitude.

"How long are you with us for?"

"Life," Smokey gave his usual hate look.

"Oh, how splendid. It's so much more worthwhile when customers book in for a long stay. Now how can we make 'life' more comfortable for you?"

A glint came into Sefton's eye. He was always forfeiting privileges for insubordination. "Well, an electric blanket would not come amiss." There was a ripple of happy laughter silenced abruptly by Mr Slughem roaring at him not to be impertinent.

"Now, now, Mr Slughem. This dear boy made a most constructive suggestion. I shall bear it in mind when the redesigning of bedrooms is put in hand."

"Cells, sir, cells," whispered Mr Slughem.

"Names are half the battle," Mr Pipplewick replied loudly and reprovingly. "From now on A Block will be known as Whites, B Block as Bucks, C Block as Boodles and D Block as Brooks. We want to make the Moor even more difficult to get into than out of, don't we, gentlemen?

"And now," said Mr Pipplewick, "let us adjourn to the dining room and try the food. I am a great believer in Delia Smith myself, but doubtless your chef is second to none, if not actually *sans pareil*. I shall sit at top table with the lifers."

It was in the middle of the meal that the whitecoated men from Broadmoor came to collect him. He had waylaid the new Governor and strangled him. As they dragged him away in his strait-jacket he turned to Mr Slughem and said, "Always remember, dear boy, stone walls do not a prison make, nor iron bars a cage."

~ *Postscript* ~

The guest from the other place leant against the pearly gates, thereby inadvertently pressing the bell. There was a clanking of keys and sliding of bolts and St Peter's head popped through the grille.

"I trust," he said, "that you are not going to try to be funny. We had a right wit here the other day whose opening gambit was, 'Trick or treat?' And only a week or two back there was this fellow who had had a mid-air collision with his mother-in-law while they were both hang-gliding. They kicked off with *Ding Dong*

Merrily on High and it wasn't even Christmas. Never mind. As St Francis always says, 'a carol is not just for Christmas, it is for life'."

"No, my good man, I hope I may call you that," said our hero, "I was minded to admire your gates and enquire after the health of the pearly Queen."

"And that," said his saintship, "is no way to speak of the Blessed Virgin. Kindly step into the antechapel and grab a pew. Hang on while I dig out your curriculum vitae. Latin, you know. You probably don't, you being C of E. Now what I really have to ask myself is how good a guest have you really been? That you tended many an English rose is recorded, but what about wallflowers? Would you consider your time on Earth as a life well lived or a life lived well?"

"One did one's best," stammered our friend.

"One's best to do what?"

"Well, to have a good time of course. At minimum expense. Thrift is a virtue, you know."

St Peter made a note of the fact. "Now, how about your good deeds?"

"Glad you asked me that," said the applicant, playing for time. Suddenly his face lit up. A flash of inspiration dawned. "I tried to save a goldfish from drowning."

"And how did you do that?"

"I put my hand in and removed it from its bowl."

"And then?"

"Then the cat came and ate it."

"That was a good deed?"

"I meant well."

"How old were you?"

"Three. Nothing since, that I can instantly recall; except that I once let Charlie Fotheringham use my second-best fishing rod."

"How about giving to charity? That you had faith and hope I doubt not, but charity is something else."

"Donkey sanctuary in Devon, Shelter, the NSPCC. I mentioned them all in my will."

"But you did not actually leave them anything?"

"No, but I mentioned them."

"How about fidelity?"

"Ah, yes. To thine own self be true."

"What of the commandments?"

"I never coveted my neighbour's ox. Even if I had a neighbour with an ox, I am sure I would have been happy for him to hang on to it."

> "Did you ... make one heap of all your winnings
> And risk it on one throw of pitch and toss
> And lose, and start again at your beginnings
> And never breathe one word about your loss?"

"Certainly not."

"Glad about that. Up here we consider this Kipling fellow to have had a screw loose."

A Brownie point at last.

"Well, Mr Guest, I would like you to think of me as a somewhat Gilbertian figure. My object all sublime, I shall achieve in time ... Follow me please."

St Peter led the guest into a small smoke-filled room infested with wall-to-wall people. The only nibbles were stuffed prunes – mountains of them carried by plain waitresses struggling to get through the crush. His fellow guests were totally beyond the pale: scientists, women with opinions, terrible deceased bores he had known back on Earth and to whom he had given the widest of all possible berths. A gnarled specimen of the wine waiter tribe approached him, "Babycham or Blue Nun, sir? I'd have the Babycham. If you ask me, the Blue Nun is corked."

"Thank you so much. Do you happen to know when these proceedings reach their conclusion?"

The grizzled old sommelier grinned toothlessly at him.

"Oh, they don't, sir. But if you atone very hard for a few hundred years you may get given parole. That means you can go down the pub on Tuesdays and Fridays and have a nice glass of warm beer with the lads. They've got telly down at the pub. You'll be able to watch the football, though I find it a bit boring. The same side always wins."

"Good gracious," said the guest, "and which side is that?"

"The Saints, of course."

"Ah, yes."

After a mere matter of weeks the Guest from Hell put in for an interview with St Peter.

"You have a problem?" said the old boy.

"Well, frankly I'd rather settle for hell."

"Forgive me. I should have explained. That cocktail party, like most, IS hell."

Amen.

"Welcome to Hell – I'm sure you know everyone..."

ANNIE TEMPEST
Tottering-by-Gently

Annie is one of Britain's best-loved cartoonists. For her popular strip cartoon 'The Yuppies', which ran for seven years in the *Daily Mail*, she was recognised by her peers in the Cartoonists Club of Great Britain as 'Strip Cartoonist of the Year'. In 1993 Annie embarked on her current internationally acclaimed cartoon strip, '*Tottering-by-Gently*' for *Country Life* Magazine. In 1995 The O'Shea Gallery was appointed agent for Annie Tempest's originals and publisher of her books and prints. The Gallery promotes and exhibits Annie's work worldwide.

Tottering-by-Gently is a village in the fictional county of North Pimmshire, in which the big house, Tottering Hall, is inhabited by Lord and Lady Tottering, affectionately known as Daffy and Dicky. Through them and their extended family, Annie Tempest casts her gimlet eye over everything from inter-generational tensions and the differing perspectives of men and women, to field sports, diet, ageing, gardening, fashion, food, convention and much, much more. Her now large international following proves that she touches a note of universal truth in her beautifully executed and exquisitely detailed cartoons as she gently laughs with us at the stuff of life.

Annie Tempest has had seven collections of her cartoons published and has worked for most of our national newspapers and life-style magazines over the last fifteen years. As Sir Roy Strong recently observed: "Annie Tempest has a great talent. She has the similar cult appeal to Osbert Lancaster and has created her characters from a certain set, but her observations are social as against political. They are gentler and beautifully observed. Annie Tempest is a bit of England – she articulates the things which set us apart and which form our identity."